DARTS

GREATEST GAMES

FIFTY FINEST MATCHES

DARTS
GREATEST GAMES
FIFTY FINEST MATCHES
MATT BOZEAT

FOREWORD BY
RAYMOND VAN BARNEVELD

First published by Pitch Publishing, 2017

Pitch Publishing
A2 Yeoman Gate
Yeoman Way
Worthing
Sussex
BN13 3QZ
www.pitchpublishing.co.uk
info@pitchpublishing.co.uk

ISBN 978-1-78531-300-4

Typesetting and origination by Pitch Publishing
Printed in Great Britain by TJ International

Contents

For my perfect little girl Carla Diana,
Lydia, Mum and Dad

Forever in my thoughts Mum

Acknowledgements

Thanks to the following for interviews – Phil Taylor, Raymond van Barneveld, Michael van Gerwen, Gary Anderson, Adrian Lewis, John Part, Martin Adams, Dennis Priestley, Bob Anderson, Ted Hankey, Andy Fordham, Jelle Klaasen, Scott Waites, Glen Durrant, Trina Gulliver, Anastasia Dobromyslova, Rod Harrington, Bobby George, Robbie Green, Chris Mason, Kevin Painter, Tony O'Shea, Andy Callaby, Andy Hamilton, James Richardson, Paul Lim, Shaun Greatbatch, Dennis Harbour – and thanks also to Matt Ward, Patrick Chaplin, Dave Allen, Paul Starr, Will Adamson, John Rawling, Jamie Caven, Hugh Asher, Steve Palmer and Adam Steel.

Foreword

I OFTEN get asked what the favourite match of my career has been, or which game I enjoyed the most, and I'm so proud that I can look back over more than 25 years and have so many great memories.

The debate about which is the greatest match ever has been spoken about a lot over the years. Maybe Keith Deller's win over Eric Bristow in 1983, or John Lowe hitting the first televised nine-dart finish, Michael van Gerwen nearly hitting two nine-darters in a row or any one of so many games involving Phil Taylor?

Coming over to the PDC in 2006 gave me my chance to play against Phil on a regular basis, and I was desperate to prove myself against the greatest player ever.

I'm proud to think that I've done that, and although Phil's won more than his share of our games since, we've got a wonderful rivalry, a great friendship and so much respect for each other.

Hopefully that's something that comes across for the fans who watch us at the events or on TV around the world, because the game has now got so big.

Darts is a fantastic sport, not just for us players to be involved in, but also for the fans, and it's amazing to see so many people coming to enjoy themselves everywhere we go.

Having so many more tournaments now, of course, means that there are so many more brilliant matches which get seen worldwide, so to pick out just 50 for this book must have been a massive job for Matt!

It's a huge honour for me that three of my wins are included; my win over Richie Burnett in the 1998 BDO World Championship final will always be so special for me – it changed my life and came three years after Richie beat me in the final. I can still remember the emotion when I won.

My 2016 World Championship win over Michael van Gerwen is included too, and it was a really memorable game for a lot of reasons. Michael has been unbelievable with what he's achieved in recent years, and to win a game like that against him at Alexandra Palace meant a lot to me.

And finally, my game with Phil to win the 2007 World Championship. Is it really ten years ago already? I was 3-0 down in sets but I didn't panic. I had to stay calm and believe in myself; the 180s came and the doubles, and then I won the sudden death leg.

The reaction in the Netherlands was unbelievable and people still talk about that game everywhere we go in the world. It makes me so proud to look at the picture of me on my office wall holding that trophy.

Raymond van Barneveld, February 2017

Phil Taylor v
Raymond van Barneveld

2009 PDC World Championship final

THE way Phil Taylor saw it, he owed Raymond van Barneveld one.

Any loss was hard to take, but that loss in the 2007 PDC World Championship final was possibly harder to take than any other.

Van Barneveld boldly said he joined the PDC to beat Taylor and he had done just that.

After that, John Part reckoned van Barneveld's was the scalp the players prized most rather than Taylor's and although Taylor said he was glad the pressure was on someone else for a change, he didn't mean it.

He wanted to be the player the others feared, the one they prayed they didn't draw in tournaments and in the two years since that World Championship final, Taylor had beaten van Barneveld five times in seven matches in front of the television cameras.

The averages were always sky high, the human drama compelling.

Of all darts' great rivalries, theirs was surely the greatest and as with all great rivalries in all sports – think Borg and McEnroe, Ali and Frazier – they were very different characters.

Both were likeable enough, but Taylor was harder, thought less; van Barneveld was more vulnerable and complex.

"Raymond won five world titles, then changed his darts," said Andy Fordham. "Why would you do that?"

Van Barneveld got disheartened sometimes, Taylor never did.

Van Barneveld would shake his head on stage when he couldn't find the answers; all Taylor ever showed was a workmanlike determination to get the job done.

From the moment van Barneveld sank the match-winning double in the World Championship final just before midnight on 1 January, 2007, Taylor's job was to get the trophy back.

That match and the rivalry between Taylor and van Barneveld helped lift darts out of the leisure centres and working men's clubs of its working-class roots.

Bigger venues were booked for the Premier League and the World Championship shifted from the Circus Tavern to the larger and distinctly more upmarket Alexandra Palace.

Neither defending champion van Barneveld nor Taylor reached the final there in 2008.

Van Barneveld was beaten by Kevin Painter in the second round and, more surprisingly, Wayne Mardle overturned a 3-0 deficit to oust Taylor in the last eight.

Their defeats cleared the way for John Part to become a three-time world champion with victory over qualifier Kirk Shepherd in the final.

Taylor had appeared in every other PDC World Championship final – all 14 of them – and perhaps darts would stride off into a sunlit future of stadia and slimmed-down superstars without him...

Shepherd looked to have a good future, Michael van Gerwen would surely break through and there were others.

The whispers about Taylor's possible demise grew louder after James Wade, Terry Jenkins and, worst of all, Peter Manley inflicted defeats on him in the opening four weeks of the following Premier League.

Taylor later admitted the loss to Manley had left him "the lowest I have ever been". Manley won convincingly 8-3, then mocked Taylor in his celebrations.

After that night in Coventry, Taylor was just about unbeatable.

He practised harder than ever, added several points to his average and won the Premier League, World Matchplay, Desert Classic, World Grand Prix, European Championship and Grand Slam of Darts.

Only van Barneveld beat him in front of the television cameras in those eight months, in the quarter-finals of the UK Open and again, the match went to a deciding leg.

In the previous round, Taylor had recorded the highest-ever televised three-dart average, a colossal 114.53 against Wes Newton, and before that he threw a nine-darter against Jamie Harvey.

Going into the 2009 PDC World Championship, Taylor joked there had been a photograph of him with the trophy on his mantelpiece for the last two years where the trophy itself usually stood.

The bookmakers reckoned the trophy was heading back to the Potteries with him, and the form he was in meant only one man was capable of stopping him ...

Taylor was seeded to meet him in the final.

Taylor dropped only three sets – and just a handful of legs – on his way there with wins over Steve Grubb (3-0), Michael van Gerwen

(4-0), Kevin Painter (4-1), Co Stompe (5-0) and Mervyn King (6-2) and van Barneveld came through the other, tougher half of the draw.

Ronnie Baxter took him to a seventh and deciding set in the third round and James Wade pushed him hard in the last four after van Barneveld had thrown the first nine-dart leg in the championship's history in his quarter-final win over Jelle Klaasen.

Somehow, Taylor had to find a way to better that. He would have a nine-darter in the final, he told himself, and he appeared in the mood to do it.

Taylor won the nearest the bull, handed the throw to van Barneveld, then raced to the opening two sets without dropping a leg. Taylor should have led 3-0, but missed three darts at a double, allowing van Barneveld to nick the set.

The fourth set would be crucial.

Remembering how he let van Barneveld back into the final two years earlier from 3-0 down, Taylor knew he couldn't allow the Dutchman to build any momentum and level the match at 2-2.

Both players found an extra gear in that fourth set.

Taylor started with five successive treble 20s – and van Barneveld responded.

There were seven maximum 180s in the opening four legs – Taylor threw four, van Barneveld three – and in the deciding leg, van Barneveld missed two chances to level the match and Taylor nailed double eight to lead 3-1.

It was the story of the match.

Van Barneveld stayed with Taylor in every fiercely competitive set that followed – until the legs when it really mattered. That was when van Barneveld missed and Taylor hit.

The fifth, sixth and eighth sets also went all the way to a deciding leg – and Taylor won the lot.

That eighth set – and the match – came to an end when Taylor nailed treble 19, then double 12 to complete an 81 checkout.

That finish gave him three-dart average of 110.94, the best in both the PDC World Championship and a PDC final.

Predictably enough, Taylor held both the previous records.

"This was so satisfying after not winning the World Championship for the last two years," said Taylor, and in the press room afterwards van Barneveld looked exasperated, close to tears.

Five of the eight sets went to a fifth and deciding leg, indicating a close match, but the score still read at the end Taylor 7, van

Barneveld 1. The score seemed cruel on van Barneveld, but he knows better than anyone that finals are won by the thrower who holds his nerve under pressure and on this occasion, that was Taylor.

"He hit everything, so what can I do?" van Barneveld told reporters. "I averaged 101.50 and still lost 7-1.

"Whatever I'm doing I can't play at that level. I don't know how to beat this man."

THE morning after the night before, Andy Fordham woke up with a trophy and absolutely no idea how he got it.

Thankfully, the newspaper headlines helped fill in the gaps in his memory...

Nobody did less to help darts clean up its 'pie and a pint and another pint' image than Fordham.

He looked like an extra from the *Not the Nine O'Clock News* sketch where 'Fat Belly' and 'Even Fatter Belly' threw darts to keep themselves occupied while waiting their turn in a drinking competition.

Fordham admitted: "The only reason I started playing darts was because there was drinking involved!

"My football team used to train on Wednesdays, then they would head to the pub to play darts. I went along to have a few beers and to watch them play. They were short of a player one night, so I stepped in. I was shit, but darts had a grip on me. I played at every opportunity. I would take my darts everywhere in case there was the chance of getting a game."

Fordham spent more and more time in pubs and had to swap the 'Whippet' nickname of his youth for something rather more appropriate. Bobby George called him 'The Viking' after an exhibition match and if he hadn't come up with the name, someone else surely would have done.

Fordham weighed a salad-dodging 30 stones, was unshaven, had hair down his back and was forever thirsty. In a film of his life, Brian Blessed was a shoo-in for the lead role.

One look at Fordham and the argument that darts is a serious sport played by self-disciplined athletes is instantly lost. But then he never pretended to be an ambassador for anything. Fordham was just being himself; an affable enough pub landlord who liked a drink.

He raised eyebrows and a few smiles in the press room during the 2004 BDO World Championship when he announced he had employed a fitness coach.

Just because darts wanted to be taken seriously and be recognised as a sport, it didn't mean Fordham had to take himself seriously.

Fordham put down his drink for long enough to qualify for the World Championships at the Lakeside Country Club in 1995 – and headed straight for the bar when he got there to prepare for his first-round match against Nicky Turner.

"It was my first time on television and I was really, really nervous," he remembered. "I drank half a bottle of brandy, a crate of Pils – and it worked. I won. So I kept doing it."

Fordham went on to reach the semi-finals, losing to Richie Burnett, and also reached the last four the following year, then again in 1999 and 2001.

Wins over Brian Derbyshire (3-1), Tony West (3-0) and Darryl Fitton (5-4) took him through to the semi-finals for a fifth time in 2004 and a match with three-time world champion Raymond van Barneveld.

Van Barneveld usually beat Fordham and was fancied to do so again. "I did an interview with Dutch television before the match and I told them I was getting closer and closer to Raymond," said Fordham. "I said he was worried about me."

At 3-0 down, Fordham's chins were on the floor.

"I thought it was all over," he admitted.

"I had nothing to lose, so I just threw darts and they went in. Raymond told a newspaper afterwards that he thought aliens had come down from space and interfered with my game during the interval, but I never felt anything."

How much had Fordham drunk before the match? "Shedloads," he said.

In the final, he would meet Mervyn King and he was an altogether different character.

He wore a 'what are you looking at' expression and, though yet to win a major ranking event, he was a world finalist in 2002, losing to Tony David, and was throwing well.

King was the width of a cigarette paper away from a nine-dart leg against Tony O'Shea in the last four at Frimley Green – and if either player was going to run out of steam in the best-of-11-sets final, it clearly wasn't going to be him.

King had breezed past O'Shea 5-1 in their semi-final, while Fordham had been taken all the way to a ninth and deciding set by van Barneveld.

The bookmakers made King the favourite – just.

"Mervyn is one of the best players I've ever seen and if he is on his game, you have to play very well to beat him," said Fordham. "But his head can go all over the place. He starts thinking about things and it affects his game."

Maybe he would start thinking about the crowd. Fordham, who had proved his big-match temperament by winning the 1999 World Masters, reckoned "98 per cent" of them were on his side and added: "It probably had an effect on Mervyn."

They cheered Fordham when he waddled on stage looking like an athlete from the ankles down – he was wearing trainers – but he didn't look like much of a darts player when he started the match with a throw of 30.

King also took a while to settle and the opening two sets went against the throw. Fordham pulled away to lead 3-1, but King, putting everything into every dart as always, drew level at 3-3.

Fordham held his throw in the seventh set to edge ahead 4-3 and the eighth set would be crucial.

It went all the way to a nerve-shredding fifth and deciding leg and with King just 80 points away from levelling the match, Fordham took aim at 139 for a break and a 5-3 lead.

Showing a sniper's nerve, 'The Viking' nailed treble 20, treble 13, double 20.

He was now only a set away from victory.

John Part, the 1994 BDO world champion, knows a decisive dart when he sees one and he told BBC viewers: "That's a heartbreaker for Mervyn."

As always, King relished the fight. He stuck his chest out, threw 140s and grabbed the opening two legs of the ninth set. But he ran out of steam and, as King's form dipped, Fordham rediscovered his fluency.

He levelled the set, then took out a scruffy 61 finish on double eight with his last dart to win the match.

Then he just stood there and sighed, trying to take it all in. Fordham was the BDO world champion and he couldn't quite believe it.

The crowd – including his underemployed fitness coach – were on their feet clapping and cheering and although King told him not to cry, Fordham had to dry his eyes on the sleeves of his XXXXXXL size shirt.

"I'm an emotional bloke," he said later.

Much of the above is news to Fordham...

Asked for his memories of the greatest night of his darts career several years later, he admitted: "I was that drunk I don't remember

it! I've seen the match on DVD and it looks like I had a great time –
and I'm sure I had an even better time after it.

"I was half-pissed all the time. I'm not proud of it. It's just what I
did to cope."

Glen Durrant v
Paul Hogan

THROUGHOUT 2016, Glen Durrant was to the BDO what Michael van Gerwen was to the PDC.

He won eight ranking titles, including a successful defence of the World Masters, and ahead of the Grand Slam of Darts, van Gerwen rated the 45-year-old from Middlesbrough as the only BDO player who had any sort of chance.

Durrant reached the last 16 at Wolverhampton Civic Hall – losing to Raymond van Barneveld 10-7 – and the expectation was that, within a few months, he would be a PDC player.

The story went, he just wanted one last stab at 'the Lakeside' before moving on.

'The Lakeside' had unhappy memories for 'Duzza'.

There was a heartbreaking semi-final loss to Martin 'Wolfie' Adams in 2015 – Durrant said it took him a month to get over the defeat – and 12 months later, history repeated itself.

"Maybe five weeks this time (to get over it)," said Durrant after missing three darts at a double to beat Scott Waites in their quarter-final.

According to the bookmakers, there would be a happier ending for him in 2017.

Durrant went into the championship as the overwhelming favourite – and taking out 167 in the opening leg of his first-round match against Nick Kenny was a good way to start.

Kenny actually went on to win that opening set, but Durrant took the next three and played Paul Hogan next.

Hogan was a 53-year-old van driver from Basingstoke known as 'Crocodile Dundee' who, though well respected on the circuit, had gone 12 years without a major ranking victory and was ranked 100th in the BDO, 99 places below Durrant.

Hogan had only just made it through to the Lakeside, surviving a match dart in the qualifiers, and once there, he threw well.

His 91.62 average against Welsh veteran Martin Phillips in the first round was his best in 14 matches on the Lakeside stage, spread over 22 years, and in the estimation of commentator John Rawling, he would need to add a few points to that if he was going to beat

Durrant over the best of seven sets. The bookmakers didn't fancy his chances of doing it – they made Durrant 4/5 to win 4-0 – but Hogan appeared to be looking forward to the match more than his opponent.

"Paul was winning the match backstage," said Durrant. "He was singing and looking so relaxed, while I had never felt so nervous.

"I had been the world No. 1 and winning events, but for the first time in my darts career, I felt there was real pressure on me.

"In every interview, I said the pressure wasn't getting to me, but I wanted to win the world title so much and the truth was, I had never felt so tight and nervous."

Hogan was known for throwing his best darts on the floor – Durrant said before the match: "If it was a local competition for 200 quid, he would probably be favourite because he is a fantastic competition player" – but this time, he took his floor form on to the big stage and put together what commentator Jim Proudfoot described as "20 minutes of fantasy darts".

He won the opening two sets without reply.

Hogan seemed to find two treble 20s most visits – certainly more often than Durrant did – and was comfortably picking off his finishes, including a jaw-dropping 140 to snatch the second leg of the opening set against the throw and an 81 shot on the bull's-eye in the next set.

Hogan only missed one dart at a double in those opening two sets, and at the interval Durrant lingered for a few moments, giving the board a long, confused look as he dragged himself slowly off stage.

"I was looking around thinking: 'How did this happen?'" he remembered. "I was a beaten man."

Durrant spent the interval gathering his thoughts and returned to break Hogan's throw in the opening leg of the third set. Hogan broke straight back – and the set went to a deciding fifth leg.

Durrant had a shot at 80 for 2-1, missed and Hogan found double top with his last dart for a 3-0 lead.

"We have an upset on now," said commentator John Rawling and moments later he gasped, "I can barely believe what I'm seeing," after Hogan took out 130 on the bull's-eye to break Durrant's throw in the opening leg of the fourth set.

Hogan then held, leaving him one leg away from the match.

"I was 3-0 down and 2-0 down," said Durrant, "and I'm known for being a frontrunner…"

Proudfoot told viewers: "Durrant has barely a puncher's chance from here," but there were signs that for Hogan, the finishing line wouldn't be reached without a wobble or two. He couldn't find a treble with his next eight darts and though he fought back to leave 11 for the match, Durrant didn't give him a shot at it, nailing double 16.

Hogan then threw for the match and after a topsy-turvy leg, he got a chance to take out 109.

Treble 19 with his first dart meant the finish was on and 20 left double 16.

He was agonisingly just inside his target and with Durrant waiting on double ten, it seemed Hogan would have to wait for another chance.

Three missed double tens from Durrant later, Hogan was back on the oche taking aim at double eight.

He threw his first dart well enough, without any signs of a twitch, but it veered millimetres off course and landed just the wrong side of the wire – in double 16.

Hogan couldn't have been any closer and while he was thinking about his misfortune, Durrant found his double, then held his throw for 3-1.

Durrant said: "At the interval, my best friend, Dennis Coleman, said to me: 'If you break his throw in the next set, you will win the match,'" while Chris Mason told viewers the match would be decided by "how long it [his missed match-winning chance] stays with him [Hogan]."

Durrant was well aware of the mental struggle his opponent was facing. He said: "At times like that, you either think: 'I'm going to get another chance and I will hit the double next time' or you think: 'I should have won this match by now and he's fighting back, what am I going to do?'"

Hogan appeared to do the latter.

There was an anguished look on his face when Durrant stole the darts off him in the opening leg and Hogan bowed his head and shouted "Come on" at himself in annoyance as the set drifted away from him.

"Paul could never be a poker player," said Durrant. "He wears his heart on his sleeve and when I saw him shaking his head, I thought: 'I can come back and win this match now.'"

Durrant won that crucial fifth set against the throw for 3-2 – and if he held in the next, he would be level at 3-3, from being 3-0 down and a dart from defeat.

Hogan fashioned half a chance to turn the match back his way in the third leg.

He left 156 for a break and after two treble 20s, he took aim at double 18.

That double had not been kind to Hogan throughout the match and again, he was just short.

Durrant sank double four for a hold, then Hogan held and in the decider, Durrant had the darts and pulled away.

He left six darts to take out 76 – and needed only three.

3-3 and Hogan shook his head. How had it come to this?

Durrant said: "The year before, I was 4-2 and 2-0 up against Scott Waites and lost, so I knew how Paul was feeling when I was fighting back – and I took a lot of inspiration from that.

"You feel like an athlete seizing up when he's close to the finishing line.

"No matter what you try, it doesn't work – and your opponent is fighting back.

"I knew how he was feeling and tried to capitalise."

Hogan had the darts in the deciding seventh set, but missed a dart at double top in the opening leg – and Durrant made no mistake with his next dart for a break that put him in the lead for the first time in the match.

There was only a dart between them in the second leg as well. Durrant missed the bull's-eye, then Hogan missed the bull's-eye to break.

Durrant couldn't take out 25 with his next three, handing Hogan the chance to put the match back in the balance.

He had two darts at double eight and again, his nerve failed him.

Hogan was furious with himself and his miss didn't go unpunished.

That put Durrant, 3-0 and 2-0 down an hour or so earlier, 2-0 up in the deciding set and around 15 good darts away from the match.

Hogan wasn't beaten yet and dragged another 180 out of himself to set up a hold of throw that kept him in the match.

He needed another big effort in the next to break and send the match into a tiebreak, but this time it proved to be beyond him.

The Durrant throw was never under any pressure and he had six darts to take out 87.

He fired in double 16 for the match.

"When I came off stage, I did think to myself: 'Maybe it's my year, I'm going to win the world title,'" said Durrant and he did win the world title, beating Danny Noppert in the final, 7-3.

"THERE are donkeys on Blackpool beach who want to watch this match," gasped Sid Waddell as world No. 1 Rod Harrington duelled with Ronnie Baxter for the World Matchplay title at the Winter Gardens.

Had they got in, the donkeys would have been rooting for Baxter.

He was the local boy – from Church, near Accrington – making a mockery of pre-tournament odds of 100/1.

On noisy nights, he toppled Phil Taylor and Chris Mason and the way he was playing, it looked like he could beat anyone.

Baxter seemed to think so.

Seasoned darts screamer Sid Waddell, in the commentary box for Sky Sports, reckoned he had "never seen such a cocky bloke".

Waddell also said Baxter had "the best eye since Jocky Wilson" – and he was fast.

Sky Sports clocked him taking between eight and nine seconds to throw his darts, making him electrifying to watch and hard to play against.

The temptation was to play at Baxter's million-miles-per-hour pace – and few were as good at it as he was.

According to the WDC, Harrington was the best player in the world and, wearing a waistcoat and a snarl, he chiselled out wins over Gary Mawson (8-6) and Bob Anderson (14-12) on his way to the final in Blackpool.

"I never thought I would lose," said Harrington, who believed matches were won and lost between the ears.

"I thought my name was on the trophy from the moment I got into my car and headed up to Blackpool."

The best-of-35-legs final had a subplot. This wasn't just Harrington v Baxter, it was WDC v BDO. At the time, BDO players were still able to compete in WDC tournaments, adding an edge to matches between players from the rival organisations.

Harrington remembered: "I saw [WDC chief executive] Dick Allix on my way to the venue and he said: 'Please win.'

"There was that extra weight on my shoulders, definitely. If Ronnie had beaten me, that would have hurt us.

"Ronnie beat Phil and thought he was the bee's knees. I said: 'You haven't beaten the best in the world. You're playing the best in the world in the final.'"

For all that, as early as the third leg, Waddell said Baxter was "going to take some beating".

But for eight legs, Harrington stayed with him as neither player missed much.

The first chance for a break came in the ninth – and Harrington put his dart just outside double seven.

Baxter had a dart at tops for a break in the next – and missed.

Baxter did break in the 14th leg, then held off Harrington's attempts to break back in the next, stepping way across the oche – "He's in Fleetwood!" joked commentator Dave Lanning – to steer his last dart into double 16.

That put Baxter three legs clear at 9-6 and he broke in the next for 10-6.

The gap was four legs – and two breaks of throw.

"I was losing but I never doubted myself, not for one minute," said Harrington. "I knew I was the world No. 1 for a reason. I was the best. I was beating players like Phil Taylor, Dennis Priestley and Bob Anderson regularly."

Harrington had a way of dealing with losing scorelines. "I didn't look at the other bloke's score," he said. "I used to just talk to my daughter in my head. I used to say: 'Come on Tori, help me out.'"

Harrington found the inspiration for a well-timed 180 that set up a break in the 17th leg for 10-7 and after Baxter missed a dart at tops – a rare miss on his favourite double – for 11-7, Harrington squeezed in double ten at the second attempt for 10-8.

The gap remained at two legs going into the break after Harrington took out 121 for 11-9.

In the 23rd leg, Harrington missed a dart at double 16 for a break, but with Baxter back on 126, it seemed likely he would come back for another shot.

Trebble 19 with his first dart meant the shot was on and Baxter followed it with a breezy 19 – and the bull's-eye.

"That will hurt Harrington," reckoned commentator John Gwynne, but he shrugged it off to hold for 13-11 and fashion the chance of a break in the 25th leg.

He took his chance to trim the gap to 13-12 and with the help of a 180, Harrington held his throw for 13-13.

"Is Ronnie starting to get rattled?" wondered Gwynne.

Harrington missed a dart at double eight for a break and 14-13, but it didn't look like being a costly miss.

Baxter was on 160 and the way he had been playing in the last couple of legs, it looked to be beyond him.

It wasn't beyond him and with two treble 20s and a double top, he turned the match back his way.

Baxter went on to get a break in the 30th leg for 16-14 after Harrington missed the bull's-eye and that left him needing to hold his throw in the 31st and 33rd legs for the match.

Baxter held in the 31st leg, Harrington replied in the next.

Before the 33rd leg, Gwynne told his audience that Baxter was "12 good darts, maybe 15" away from the title.

His first three landed in treble 20, treble 20 and treble one – but he made a mess of his next two visits.

Baxter followed that opening 123 with scores of 81 and 41 – and Harrington stole the darts off him with three successive 140s, leaving 81 after nine.

He found the double nine he needed, but his dart dramatically dropped out of the board, gifting Baxter a chance at 156 for the match.

He left 64 and got a shot at it after Harrington missed again.

Baxter ended up getting a dart at double top – and pulled it a centimetre or more below the target.

Harrington held his nerve, finding double four with his last dart for a break that put him just a leg behind at 17-16.

The 34th leg was similarly nip and tuck and Harrington won it with a last dart double eight with Baxter sitting on 56 for the match.

That levelled the scores at 17-17 and sent the match into a tiebreak.

Baxter had the throw in the 35th leg and, after 15 darts, he left 40 with Harrington on 125.

"The usual route is to go for 25 with your first dart," said Harrington. "I thought I might miss 25, but I knew I wouldn't miss 15.

"I didn't mean to hit the treble…"

That left 80 and Gwynne told viewers: "He's got to get another treble…"

Maybe not.

Harrington smirked briefly as he weighed up his options. There seemed to be only one. Eighty with two darts had always meant treble 20, double ten.

"The doubles are bigger than the trebles," said Harrington years later, "and when you're on 80, two double tops is the way to go. It makes sense, but nobody had done it before in a televised tournament. I hadn't even done it myself in practice…"

To the surprise of everyone – including the cameraman who was zooming in on treble 20 – Harrington put his next dart in double top – and his third alongside it.

"When the second double top went in, I gave it large," was how Harrington remembers his celebration.

"I thought: 'That will hurt him.' I took my darts out of the board and as I was walking back, I noticed Ronnie looking at me, so I said: 'What a cracking shot!'

"I knew I had him."

After 90 minutes of chasing Baxter, Harrington was finally ahead – and a hold of throw away from winning the match.

Harrington outscored Baxter, leaving six darts to take out 140 and hit double five to win what Gwynne called "a match in a million".

Harrington said afterwards: "I hope they put it in the archives and show it time and time again."

Even better, it's in this book!

Raymond van Barneveld
v James Richardson

2012 PDC World Championship first round

WHEN interviewed before the 2012 PDC World Championship, Raymond van Barneveld told reporters he was feeling relaxed, throwing well – and that he had never heard of James 'Ruthless' Richardson, his opponent in the first round.

Paul Nicholson, Simon Whitlock and Michael van Gerwen knew all about him. Richardson had beaten them all in PDC Tour events during an impressive first year on the circuit and, he reckoned, he would beat van Barneveld as well at Alexandra Palace on his television debut.

Richardson had earned enough money on the tour to qualify and had rather more belief in himself than the bookmakers who made him a 1,500/1 outsider for the World Championship, held by Adrian Lewis.

"As soon as the draw was made, I was sure I would beat him," said Richardson.

"I knew I would beat him. Lots of players suffer with nerves, but I wasn't nervous. I was in good form and I liked playing the big boys and showing them what I could do."

Richardson, previously a leg away from qualifying for the BDO World Championship, was a 37-year-old bricklayer from Rushden in Northamptonshire who had started playing in the local pubs with father Chris when he was "12 or 13" years old.

He was a quarter-finalist at the World Youth Championship in his teens, but his darts CV clearly didn't compare with van Barneveld's.

Though the Dutchman's form wasn't great in 2011, he had still won five world titles and on the advice of Eric Bristow, Rod Harrington and others, van Barneveld had switched back to using the darts that toppled Phil Taylor in the 2007 World Championship final.

For his best-of-five-sets, first-round match with Richardson, he wore a new pink shirt and was clean-shaven. Proof, reckoned the experts, that van Barneveld was feeling good about himself and the thinking was, a van Barneveld who feels good about himself is harder to beat than that other, slightly unkempt, troubled van Barneveld who sometimes turns up in his place. Harrington, who knows as much about form and the players as anyone, predicted van Barneveld would win 3-0.

Everyone else thought van Barneveld would win 3-0 too – apart from Richardson.

Richardson got the crowd of 2,500 revellers on his side – they sang along heartily to 'Vindaloo', chosen in recognition of his love of curry – if only for a minute or so.

Their true allegiance was revealed when van Barneveld appeared. "The crowd did love 'Vindaloo'," said Richardson, "but then all I could hear was everyone chanting 'Barney Army'.

"I thought: 'There's only one way to shut them up. I've got to show them what I can do.'"

In the opening leg, van Barneveld didn't let his many supporters down.

Van Barneveld, never beaten in the first round of the PDC World Championship since crossing darts' divide in 2006, answered Richardson's opening throw of 100 with a maximum 180 and went on to wrap up the leg in 12 darts with a 130 checkout, an impressive statement of intent.

Van Barneveld, smoothly, effortlessly sliding his darts into the trebles and doubles, held his throw in the next leg and looked close to his best, but Richardson didn't notice.

He said: "I didn't watch him throwing. I just got my head down and didn't look at what he was doing. I've always done that. I play the board, not the player, no matter who I'm playing. I just told myself to keep pounding the treble 20 as often as I could."

Richardson, a bustling, breezy thrower, held his throw in the third leg, but if he didn't take out 145 in the next leg he seemed certain to lose the set.

The way van Barneveld was throwing, 82 looked well within his range, but he didn't get a shot at it.

Richardson nailed treble 20, treble 15, double top, all in the middle, for a spectacular 145 checkout.

He held in the next as well to set up a deciding leg. Van Barneveld had the darts, but so poorly did he throw them, Richardson could afford to be rather less than 'Ruthless', missing five darts at doubles eight, four and two before finding double one for the opening set.

The 'Barney Army' were hushed.

Van Barneveld started the second set with 46, couldn't take out 58 and Richardson broke. He then held his own – his fifth successive leg – to take a grip on the match.

Van Barneveld held in the next leg, but to win the set, he had to break Richardson's throw twice and he was playing too well for that.

Richardson wrapped up the second set by moving up the 20 bed – hitting treble, single and double – for a 120 finish and remembers hearing sections of the crowd chanting his name as he left the stage. The rest probably didn't even know his name.

In an attempt to change his fortunes, van Barneveld changed his flights during the interval – and raced to the opening two legs of the third set, breaking in the first leg in just 11 darts.

But the set-winning double was harder to find.

In the third leg, van Barneveld missed darts at the bull's-eye, then double eight and double four, allowing Richardson to hold.

Still, van Barneveld had the throw in the fourth leg and left himself 65 with Richardson on 145. For the second time in the match, Richardson, throwing what commentator Stuart Pyke described as "adrenaline-pumped darts", found treble 20, treble 15, double 20 to snatch the leg to gasps from the crowd.

That sent the third set into a deciding fifth leg and if van Barneveld was going to stay in the match, he had to break Richardson's throw.

Van Barneveld's fifth 180 of the match gave him a chance, but when he went for his doubles, his aim wasn't as good.

Van Barneveld missed the bull's-eye for 167, then two more at double eight and Richardson polished off 41 in two darts – nine and double 16 – to wrap up what commentators described as "the biggest shock in the history of the PDC World Championship".

Richardson had to ring his boss to tell him he wouldn't be back at work for another day, but the adventure was ended by Kim Huybrechts in the second round.

The Belgian was a 4-1 winner, but still, Richardson headed back to the building site as a hero.

"Everyone was pleased for me," he remembered. "I was shaking hands for weeks afterwards."

Even van Barneveld started to recognise him.

"He said before we played that he didn't know who I was," said Richardson, "but that was rubbish. I had been on the tour for a year and had beaten some good players.

"He knew who I was after the match. Whenever I've seen him afterwards, he always stops to shake my hand and have a chat.

"I still watch the match now and again when I'm on a downer. I have to laugh at the comments they were making on television. They didn't think I had the balls to go up there and beat him."

Raymond van Barneveld
v Richie Burnett

1998 BDO World Championship final

BERT Vlaardingerbroek was the first Dutchman to qualify for the World Darts Championship.

No, me neither.

In 1988, he lost in the first round to Northern Ireland's Fred McMullan and in three further visits to the Lakeside, Vlaardingerbroek didn't win a match.

One match he did win was against a teenage Raymond van Barneveld and after the 3-0 victory, van Barneveld's father, Roy, shook Vlaardingerbroek's hand and told him: "Well done, Raymond didn't have a chance against you."

The words resonated with van Barneveld and he remembered in his autobiography *Barney*: "The same day I went home and trained for five hours non-stop in my room. And the day after that again and then again and again. I kept going at it constantly until eventually I started to beat Vlaardingerbroek."

The need to prove himself motivated van Barneveld – and so did money. Growing up, the van Barnevelds – parents Roy and Anneke and younger sister Bianca – lived near Den Haag's football ground, but though Raymond was a supporter, his family could never afford a ticket.

"When I grow up mum, I want to be rich," Raymond would tell Anneke and he wasn't going to get rich cleaning up at a hospital or working as a postman, jobs he held after leaving school.

Maybe van Barneveld could earn his fortune playing darts…

He was "six or seven" years old when he discovered darts during a family holiday in Mallorca. Van Barneveld remembered a fairground stall that offered a prize to anyone who could hit playing cards pinned to a wall and, more often than not, he walked away clutching a teddy or a toy. For his 17th birthday, van Barneveld was given a dartboard and some money that he invested in a set of darts.

He remembered that as the moment his darts career "accelerated", and in 1990 he pushed world champion Phil Taylor close in the European Cup in Malta.

Taylor won 4-2 after van Barneveld missed four darts at a double to send the match into a deciding seventh leg and impressed BDO bosses handed the Dutchman a wild card to play in the following year's World Championship.

At Frimley Green, he was whitewashed by Keith Sullivan in the first round after averaging just 74.88 and spent the journey home wondering how he would explain himself.

Defeats really hurt van Barneveld and no defeat hurt more than his loss in the 1995 BDO world final.

Beating Richie Burnett, from the same Welsh valleys as Leighton Rees and Alan Evans, may well have changed van Barneveld's life. But he lost and went back to delivering the post. "I was hoping to stop my job," he said, "but no sponsors came forward. People used to shout 'one hundred and eighty!' at me as I was doing my rounds."

The loss to Burnett seemed to take something out of van Barneveld and for the following two years, he didn't get beyond the second round in Frimley Green, losing to Matt Clark and Les Wallace respectively.

Van Barneveld being van Barneveld, he started thinking he was the victim of a jinx.

He turned up for the 1998 BDO World Championship wearing a necklace that belonged to "a friend who passed away" as a lucky charm and apparently full of confidence. He was the No. 1 seed and said later: "I knew I could do it."

The difficult second-round hurdle was cleared in some style. From 2-0 down to Andy Fordham, van Barneveld won nine of the next ten legs for a 3-2 win and he went on to wallop 1996 BDO world champion Steve Beaton 5-0 and Colin Monk 5-3 to reach the final, upping his average in each match.

After every win, van Barneveld, sleepy-eyed and well fed, spread himself across the BBC sofa and told the nation slowly, quietly and with real conviction that he would meet Burnett in the final and that he would beat him. "There's only one final I want and that's Richie," he said, "and I want to win 6-3."

That was the scoreline in the Welshman's favour when they had met in the final three years earlier and more recently, Burnett had also beaten van Barneveld in the World Masters.

Even so, Burnett admitted van Barneveld was "the man to beat in 1998. We were the best two players around at the time. But I was never bothered about playing anyone. If I played my best I knew I could beat all of them and the more you think about who you're playing, the more you feel the pressure."

Burnett reached the final – his third in four years – with wins over Marshall James, Kevin Painter, Peter Johnstone and Roland Scholten and the five million viewers who watched the final live on Dutch television saw two players who threw their darts very differently.

Van Barneveld was a rhythm player and when he found his rhythm, it seemed he could put his darts wherever he wanted without too much thought.

In contrast, Burnett concentrated hard on every single dart, fixing his hard eyes on his target for a few seconds before throwing.

When winning doubles were hit, Burnett would turn to the crowd, shout and bounce on the balls of his feet. "My way of handling the pressure is to be aggressive," he would explain, while van Barneveld was rather more sensitive. Win or lose, there were often tears and as van Barneveld admitted himself, sometimes he would think too much.

There were times when van Barneveld seemed to be thinking: "Am I good enough to win?" But in 1998, he had real reason to believe in himself. He was the No. 1 seed, was winning matches and if that wasn't enough, he had his lucky necklace to help him through the tough moments in matches.

Burnett, who 'dabbled' in boxing when he was younger, didn't need lucky charms.

He knew what it took to win – and lose – a World Championship final and predicted: "The best player has to be mentally tougher than anyone else and I'm pretty good at that." He also reckoned the champion would be whoever "hits the double with his last dart when he needs it". Again, Burnett fancied he was pretty good at that.

Not in the opening two sets of the final he wasn't. Burnett missed way too many doubles and van Barneveld went 2-0 up. Burnett hit back to level at 2-2 and the to-and-fro tungsten tossing went on. Van Barneveld broke for 3-2, missed three darts at a double for 4-2 and Burnett tied the scores at 3-3. The Welshman held his throw for 4-3 and before the start of the eighth set, van Barneveld kissed his necklace for luck. He knew he had to hold his throw – and he did.

The eighth set went all the way to the deciding leg – the fourth successive set to do so – and with the momentum behind him, van Barneveld breezed to the ninth without reply for a break and a 5-4 lead.

If van Barneveld held his throw in the tenth set, he would be world champion. But he couldn't.

Burnett broke to send the match into a deciding 11th set that had to be won by two clear legs.

If the score reached 5-5, there would be a sudden death deciding leg to determine both the World Championship – and whether Burnett would tie the knot.

Girlfriend Angie Oram told reporters the couple would be married if Burnett won the title again, and in the fourth leg Richie was three well-placed darts away from getting down on one knee.

He left 102 for the match, but missed the treble 14 that would have given him a dart at double top for the championship.

Van Barneveld levelled at 2-2 to send the match into a tiebreak.

The pressure was on Burnett to hold his throw and when he threw wide of double 20 and double ten that gave van Barneveld a chance – and he took it: picking off 66 in two darts for a break that left him one leg away from the match.

He couldn't finish 120 for the championship – his score of 44 left 76 – and Burnett cranked up the pressure with 100 to leave 60.

Van Barneveld found the treble 20 with his first dart, then took aim at double eight for the match – and missed.

But he didn't miss by much and, using that dart as a marker, he slid his last between the double eight wires.

Van Barneveld dropped to his knees, clutched his face and sobbed.

He would later write: "The sheer knowing that you are now a world champion, so proving to everyone that you could do it, overwhelmed me."

Bizarrely, the theme from *Star Wars* played as van Barneveld, wearing a trilby hat with a card that read 'I Love Darts' shoved into its brim, held the trophy aloft.

Burnett would say he had "given it away" and had "got cheesed off" by van Barneveld repeatedly finding the double with his last dart, while the new champion reckoned his victory would be "good for darts in Holland".

How good his win was for Dutch darts van Barneveld discovered when he arrived home at Schiphol Airport in Amsterdam – and 10,000 people were waiting to greet him.

"I can't believe there are people out there who want to be Raymond van Barneveld," he would say.

As for the necklace? "I had to stop wearing it," said van Barneveld. "I was blaming the necklace when I lost."

Trina Gulliver v Francis Hoenselaar

ANYONE for tennis? Not Trina Gulliver. She preferred darts – and at times, she wondered whether she had made the right choice.

"I'm not saying I would have been world No. 1 at tennis," she said before the 2007 BDO Women's World Championship got under way, "but I am sure I would have been earning more money.

"There can't be any five times world champions who don't earn more than me.

"The prize money is ridiculous when you compare it to the men."

The prize for the men's champion was £70,000, while the winner of the women's event picked up a cheque for £6,000, a figure described as "derisory" by Gulliver, who represented Warwickshire at tennis and the javelin – "I was good at anything to do with my arm!" – before deciding the great outdoors wasn't really for her.

Worse still, the sponsors of the Bavaria World Darts Trophy had pulled out, meaning a major tournament was lost.

The women's game appeared to be in crisis.

Part of the problem was Gulliver herself. She was just too good, dominating the World Championship since it was introduced by the BDO in 2001.

Everyone knew Gulliver would win the World Championship – and she would probably beat Francis Hoenselaar, a Dutch thrower who looked not unlike the Roxette singer's mum, in the final.

They had contested four of the six world finals at the Lakeside Country Club – and Gulliver had won them all.

By 2007, Gulliver and Hoenselaar were well established as numbers one and two in the women's game with Gulliver, from Southam in Warwickshire, some way ahead of her closest rival.

They reckoned they had met in more than 50 finals on the women's circuit and Gulliver had won more than she had lost.

"There was a spell when we dominated the circuit completely," remembered Gulliver, "and we became good friends.

"We wanted to rip each other's heads off when we played, but as soon as it was over, we would have a drink together and talk through the game.

"I think we helped each other by doing that. We would talk to each other about different shots."

To nobody's surprise, Gulliver and Hoenselaar met in the World Championship final in 2007, though both had their wobbles on their way through.

Gulliver started her world title defence against Dutch teenager Carla Molema, the world youth champion, with jittery throws of 41, 59 and 28, hinting that this year might be a struggle for 'The Golden Girl'.

She put her next three darts in the treble 20, but Molema wasn't easy to shake off and had she held her throw in the deciding leg of the second set, the match would have gone to a deciding third set.

Gulliver instead went through 2-0, then eased through her semi-final against Anastasia Dobromyslova by the same scoreline after the Russian lost her composure on crucial doubles, allowing Gulliver to record a 13th straight whitewash at the Lakeside.

In the other half of the draw, Hoenselaar was some way short of her best against American Carol Forwood in their quarter-final, blaming the lengthy journey from Holland for her poor showing, and also dropped a set to Apylee Jones in the last four.

Gulliver had averaged around ten points more than Hoenselaar on her way to the final and, given the history between them on the Lakeside stage, had to be the favourite to win the best-of-three-sets final.

But Hoenselaar gave the many Dutch fans in the crowd hope this would be different by holding her throw in a high-quality opening leg.

She took out a 151 finish after they swapped 140s, then Gulliver held and the set went to a deciding leg after a topsy-turvy fourth when Hoenselaar pinched the darts off Gulliver, then let her back.

Gulliver had a shot at the bull's-eye for the opening set against the throw, but missed and Hoenselaar found double eight for 1-0.

The pressure was now on Gulliver. She had to hold her throw in the second set to stay in the match against an opponent who was taking her half-chances.

Gulliver had come from behind to win finals before – she lost the opening set of both the 2001 and 2002 finals, to Mandy Solomons and Hoenselaar respectively – and responded well, holding her throw in 14 and 15 darts. She wrapped up the set and levelled the match with a break in the fourth leg, taking out 75 after Hoenselaar missed a dart at double top in another leg when they matched each other dart for dart.

Hoenselaar got the deciding set under way and Gulliver, throwing aggressive darts that hit the board hard, broke in the opening leg, then held for 2-0 and had the darts for the match.

With the game almost lost, Hoenselaar rediscovered her best form, leaving 85 after 12 darts to set up a break of throw that put the match back in the balance going into the fourth leg.

Either Hoenselaar held her throw to set up a deciding leg – or Gulliver broke and was champion again.

Hoenselaar had the first shot at a double – and missed.

Gulliver then had a dart at double top for the match – and missed.

Hoenselaar didn't miss again, finding double ten with her second dart, and the Women's World Championship final was going to a deciding leg.

Gulliver won the nearest the bull – neither player was that near – and started with scores of 100, 140 and 140. "She's gone up a gear," was how commentator Tony Green put it and Hoenselaar couldn't go with her.

Gulliver left herself 36 after 12 darts and took aim at double 18 for the World Championship.

She was just too high with her first dart… and her second… and her third.

That handed Hoenselaar a (long) shot at 147 for the match. The way she was finishing, it was a possibility, if a remote one.

Hoenselaar put her first dart in treble 20, then took a step back and a deep breath before aiming at treble 17.

She missed by millimetres and went on to leave 60, but didn't get a throw at it.

Gulliver put her next dart in double 18.

She said afterwards: "I looked at the trophy a couple of times during the match and thought: 'I want to take that back home.'

"But at times I thought it wasn't going to be."

IT took Martin 'Wolfie' Adams 15 years to win the World Masters and if he found winning the trophy hard, he would find keeping it even harder.

The record books showed that since the tournament started in 1974, only Eric Bristow and Bob Anderson had successfully defended the title.

That was the challenge facing Adams in Bridlington in 2009 having 12 months earlier lifted the trophy after edging out Scott Waites in a seesaw final that went all the way to the fourth leg of the 13th and deciding set.

Robbie Green, known as 'Kong' for his salad-dodging physique, headed to the Yorkshire coast that week unemployable, newly single and skint.

"I left the wife the day I drove up to Bridlington," he remembered. "It was great, the best feeling I've ever had, but she took everything. I only had £18.

"I was unemployed at the time – and pretty unemployable. All I wanted to do was play darts. My car got a flat tyre on the way up there. I rang Stephen Bunting and he was a few miles behind me so he came and picked me up. It was chaos."

The World Masters followed the qualifiers for the World Championship in Bridlington.

Green had never reached the televised stages of the World Championship before and missed out again at the qualifiers, but there was still a chance for the 35-year-old from Wallasey on the Wirral, if only a slim one.

The winner of the World Masters would also qualify, but given that Green had to slog his way through "six or seven matches" on the floor just to reach the last 32, it seemed unlikely.

But he made it through to the last 32 and when he reached the televised stages, 'Kong' kept winning.

Green, hitting a big treble most visits and finding any finish of 80 or above within his range, ousted Daryl Gurney and Ross Montgomery in sizeable upsets, then took out Connie Finnan and Lourence Ilagan to reach his first major final.

There he would meet the defending champion over the best of 13 sets, each set the best of three legs.

Adams missed four chances to break throw in the opening leg – and they looked costly misses. Green grabbed the first set and went 2-0 up with no-nonsense finishes of 130 and 81.

Minutes later, Green was a dart away from 3-0. He left 44 in the deciding leg, but pushed two darts at double 16 just outside the wire and, under huge pressure, Adams found the double ten for 2-1.

Soon, it was 2-2, but Green responded.

He held for 3-2 – winning the set by taking out 101 with Adams sitting on 22 – and the sixth also went Green's way, against the throw.

He polished off the set with a two-dart, 82 finish – bull's-eye, double 16 – and left the stage for an interval that really he could have done without.

"I'm a rhythm player," said Green, "and when I'm in my rhythm, I like to keep going."

Nevertheless, he returned to win the seventh set – in the deciding leg – for 5-2 and even for Adams, a player renowned for digging himself out of holes, the situation was looking desperate.

There were a maximum of six sets left – and he had to win five of them, three against the darts.

In four previous attempts, Adams had only broken Green's throw once, but by starting the eighth set with 137, he showed he was up for the challenge.

Green answered with 177 and stayed with the defending champion.

Adams got one dart at double 16 to hold his throw with Green on 40 – and 'Wolfie' held his nerve. Adams then broke in the next leg for 5-3.

In the ninth set, Green rushed his doubles a bit, a sign the finishing line was creeping into his thoughts, but with Adams struggling to find his trebles, 'Kong' could afford a miss or two.

He won the set without reply for 6-3, leaving him a set away from the match, and the crowd chanted: "Robbie! Robbie!"

The tenth set, a set Adams had to win, went to a deciding third leg.

Green had a shot at 144 for the title, scored 80 and came back for 64, guaranteeing him at least one dart for the match, unless he suffered a bounce-out or a meltdown.

His dart at double 16 for the match was half an inch away and Adams stuck his next dart in double five for 6-4.

"My bottle went," said Green, rather more quietly spoken and thoughtful than you might expect of someone who has his nickname tattooed on his neck. "I pulled it."

Adams would say one of the keys to darts is, "You have to forget about it when you miss," and that was the challenge now facing Green.

He had to clear his thoughts and forget about that missed double 16 and what it had cost him: a major title, £20,000 and a place at the World Championship.

Green had the throw in the 11th set, but was off target at tops and Adams, with the aid of a good marker, put his last dart in the same target for a break in the opening leg.

He then raced to the set with a 12-darter and, from 6-3 down, Adams had reduced the gap to 6-5 – and he had the throw in the 12th set.

David Croft, commentating on the match for the BBC, described Adams as a "walking, hairy soap opera". He found ways to win matches he seemed sure to lose – and he would also lose matches from winnable positions.

As for Green, he mopped his face with an extra large towel and smiled at the sheer madness of it all.

What a few days it had been and now this…

Since Green had missed a dart to win the match 7-3, he hadn't won a leg.

Green hadn't done an awful lot wrong. It was just that the half-chances he had been snaffling up earlier were being missed – and Adams had upped his game and was taking his.

"He could sniff blood," was how Green put it, "and really went for it.

"I had felt in control for so much of the match, then it turned and I was trying to stay with him in the legs. All of a sudden, it felt like I was chasing him. I was getting tired up there. Mentally, playing darts for three days takes it out of you. I was feeling pretty cabbaged."

Adams kept taking his chances, racing to the 12th set without reply for 6-6 and the crowd who had chanted Green's name minutes earlier, were now behind Adams.

Green had the throw in the deciding 13th set that had to be won by two clear legs and started with 34.

He recovered to get a shot at 65, but by now his darts were falling on the wrong side of the wires and he bust his score, putting his last dart in 13 when he aimed at neighbouring double four.

Adams was throwing too well to miss and took out 66 in two darts – bull's-eye, double eight – for a break of throw.

He could sniff the finishing line and scores of 140 and 136 took him closer.

Adams got his target down to 38 with Green way back on 204 and with his second dart, he found double 19 for the match.

Gary Anderson v
Michael van Gerwen

2017 PDC World Championship final

MICHAEL van Gerwen had a way of describing what he did in 2016.

He said it was "not normal" to win 25 PDC tournaments – and reckoned his World Championship semi-final against Raymond van Barneveld in 2017 was "not normal" either.

Van Barneveld averaged 109.34, enough to win any normal match, and was blown away 6-2.

Van Gerwen had an average of 114.05, the best at the World Championship, better than Phil Taylor's 111.21 against Shayne Burgess way back in 2002.

Comparisons between Taylor and van Gerwen were inevitable and made often.

Van Gerwen said during the 2017 World Championship: "I think I am playing better than Phil ever has. I did something incredible [in 2016] and look how well everyone's playing."

Van Gerwen was dominating an era when three-figure averages were almost commonplace, while supporters of Taylor argued his success spanned three decades and, even in his mid-fifties, he was still competitive at the highest level.

He beat van Gerwen five times in 2016, more than any other player.

Taylor made a quarter-final exit from Alexandra Palace, losing a match to old rival van Barneveld he might well have won, and van Gerwen and Anderson, the world No. 1 and world champion respectively, didn't have entirely smooth routes through to the final.

"People want to do a little bit more against me," reckoned van Gerwen and Cristo Reyes (106.07) and Darren Webster (99.20) threw big averages at him at Alexandra Palace.

Reyes was only 25 points away from taking their second-round game to a deciding seventh set when van Gerwen nailed the match-winning double.

In the other half of the draw, Dave Chisnall threw 21 180s at defending champion Gary Anderson – equalling the record set by van Barneveld in the 2007 world final – and still lost his quarter-final to the Scot in a match-of-the-tournament contender.

Anderson went on to beat consistent Peter Wright in the last four, while van Gerwen powered past van Barneveld in a match that Sky Sports commentator Rod Studd described as "darts' four-minute mile moment", such was its bar-raising quality.

Those results meant that, for the first time since 2009, when Taylor beat van Barneveld, the World Championship final would be played out by the top two seeds.

The gap between them was huge, however. Van Gerwen was way ahead of Anderson – and even further ahead of everyone else.

His 'A' game was untouchable – opponents were lucky to get a shot at a three-figure finish on their own throw – and even his 'B' and 'C' games were usually enough.

He thought fast, threw fast and such was his confidence, van Gerwen usually went for crowd-pleasing bull's-eye finishes, even when he was so far ahead of his opponent that there was no need to.

Van Gerwen was winning everything, apart from the World Championship.

"I want to throw all the other ones in the bin for this one," he said after van Barneveld beat him in the third round in 2016.

Van Gerwen had got his hands on the trophy he prized most only once – in 2014 – while Anderson went into the final with a third successive World Championship in his sights.

He had won 17 consecutive matches on the Alexandra Palace stage and though he was a Scot playing in London, it was his name the crowd chanted before a match that was of the highest quality from the start.

The opening two sets produced ten maximum 180s and at 1-1, Anderson was the happier of the two after van Gerwen blew two chances to break his throw in the second set.

The third set had a pair of 11-darters, seven perfect darts from van Gerwen – and a twist at the end.

Anderson snatched it on double 12 after van Gerwen had been wayward with two darts at double 16 for a hold.

Anderson had the darts in the fourth set for 3-1 and with both players' throws unbreakable, it went to a deciding fifth leg.

They traded big scores – Anderson threw 171, van Gerwen fired in another maximum – and the set would be decided by whether van Gerwen could find double seven, nobody's favourite double, with his last dart.

Hit it and the match was tied at 2-2, miss and van Gerwen was sure to fall 3-1 behind.

Anderson was sitting on 28. Van Gerwen flung that last dart into double seven – and celebrated like a lunatic. This was what he meant when he talked about "doing the right thing at the right time".

Anderson fashioned chances to break in the opening leg of the fifth set, but missed twice and van Gerwen didn't look back, winning the set without reply to edge ahead 3-2.

The sixth set proved to be crucial.

Van Gerwen broke Anderson's throw in the third leg after the Scot missed double 12, then held for the set.

For much of the match, there had only been a dart or two between them, but van Gerwen was now 4-2 up and had the throw in the seventh set. Anderson got down to two-dart finishes in the opening two legs – and didn't get a shot at either as van Gerwen picked off the winning doubles. He went on to wrap up the set with a brilliantly breezy 125 finish on outer bull's-eye, treble 20, double top.

Van Gerwen was 5-2 up after winning 12 of the previous 13 legs – and to stay in touch, Anderson had to hold his throw in the eighth set.

He couldn't. Van Gerwen was playing too well and polished off a 100 checkout for 6-2, leaving him one set away.

Van Gerwen did dip a bit in the ninth set, but still got a shot at 115 for the title in the fourth leg.

As he took aim, a prankster leapt from the crowd on to the stage, grabbed the Sid Waddell Trophy and headed for van Gerwen before security bundled him off stage.

His concentration broken, van Gerwen was unable to put the finishing touches to his night's work and, incredibly, Anderson came back.

He clinched the set after throwing another maximum 180 and, if he held his throw in the tenth set, the gap would be trimmed to 6-4 and the impossible would feel possible.

Anderson won the opening leg in 11 darts, van Gerwen pegged him back with an 11-darter of his own, then Anderson held and the crowd, hoping for a miracle, chanted the champion's name.

Van Gerwen silenced them with a 100 checkout – his fifth ton-plus finish of the match – to send the set into a deciding fifth leg.

Anderson had the throw and they traded 180s – the 41st and 42nd of the match, a record – but the champion made a pig's ear of a 134 finish, handing van Gerwen a shot at 85 for the match.

He couldn't find treble 15 or treble 20 with his first two darts, but the singles were enough to leave the bull's-eye and with Anderson sitting on 50, van Gerwen had to go for it. He fired his last dart into the bull's-eye for the World Championship.

"I worked so hard for this," said van Gerwen afterwards as tears rolled down his face.

Michael van Gerwen v Gary Anderson

MICHAEL van Gerwen and Gary Anderson had plenty of previous...

Anderson reckoned Lady Luck gave van Gerwen a helping hand to overturn a 3-1 deficit when they met in the third round of the PDC World Championship in 2014 – and would refer to the match as a turning point in his career.

"I'm not throwing matches away again," he promised in the aftermath of that defeat and took great satisfaction from his semi-final win over van Gerwen at Alexandra Palace the following year before going on to lift the Sid Waddell Trophy with victory over Phil Taylor.

Anderson also beat van Gerwen in the Premier League final, but the Dutchman hoovered up the UK Open, World Matchplay and Grand Slam of Darts titles.

The rivalry between them was described as "among the most intriguing in elite sport" by the *Guardian* and they brought out the best in each other.

There was a match on the PDC Tour when Anderson averaged 111 – and lost.

Van Gerwen averaged an unbeatable 117 – and did it again when he met Anderson in the final of the German Championships.

No match they ever played was more dramatic than the final of the European Championship in 2015 in Hasselt, Belgium.

Van Gerwen was the defending champion and posted three-figure averages in wins over Jeffrey de Zwaan (100.37), Cristo Reyes (106.81), Dave Chisnall (106.55) and Peter Wright (104.76) that took him through to the final.

There he met Anderson and judging by his average in his semi-final win over Adrian Lewis – an eyebrow-raising 106.26 – the Scot appeared to be playing close to his peak.

The opening legs were of the highest quality and in the fourth, van Gerwen was a whisker away from perfection.

He threw seven treble 20s, treble 19 – and then dragged his ninth dart just inside double 12.

He came back to mop up double six for a ten-darter.

After eight legs, and as many maximum 180s, the match was in the balance with the score at 4-4 and neither player able to break.

Anderson edged 5-4 ahead with another hold and both threw 180s in the tenth leg as they fought fiercely for control of the match.

Both had one dart at double top for the leg. Van Gerwen missed and Anderson hit for the first break of the match and a 6-4 lead.

He held for 7-4, then had a shot at 96 for 8-4, but couldn't do it and van Gerwen stayed in touch with a hold.

Van Gerwen kept holding – there was a spectacular 107 checkout in the 14th leg – but wasn't getting any chances to break.

Anderson was playing too well on his throw for that – he was effortlessly putting his darts in the treble 20 – and at 9-6 ahead, he was just a couple of legs away.

He would have the throw in the 17th, 19th and, if needed, the 21st leg as well.

Chris Mason can read a darts match as well as anyone and he thought van Gerwen pulling off the comeback of all comebacks was highly unlikely. He told ITV viewers it would take nine-darters to break Anderson's throw and, as well as van Gerwen was throwing, he wasn't throwing that well.

Van Gerwen did get a glimpse of a break in the 17th leg. He stole the darts off Anderson early, but then started to hit singles to let him back in and Anderson held with a 101 checkout on double 19 for 10-7.

Only one leg away now…

That left van Gerwen having to hit everything – and hope for an Anderson wobble.

The Dutchman held his throw in the 18th leg – polishing it off with a no-nonsense 78 checkout in two darts – and in the next, Anderson threw for the match.

Astonishingly, with the title only around 15 good throws away, a chink appeared in his previously chinkless throw and his aim deserted him.

He was pushing his darts, reckoned commentator Stuart Pyke, and whatever the explanation, they weren't landing where he wanted them to.

Anderson had throws of 92, 60, 91 and 94, allowing van Gerwen to pinch the throw off him.

He got to a finish first and needed only two darts to take out 62 for a match-saving break of throw.

With that break, van Gerwen was back in the match at 10-9, but three darts later, it looked as though he may have blown his chance.

He started the 20th leg with only 57, but that poor score went unpunished by Anderson.

He could manage only 81 and van Gerwen surged away with scores of 140 and 180.

Double 16 levelled the match at 10-10.

Anderson had the throw in the deciding leg and they were neck and neck – until Anderson threw 84 and van Gerwen replied with 145 to get first shot at a checkout.

Van Gerwen took 85 off 160 to leave 75 – and Anderson took aim at 134 for the match.

He didn't get anywhere near a shot at the match-winning double and van Gerwen fired in treble 17 and double 12 to win the match and complete an astonishing Houdini act.

Six minutes earlier, Anderson had led 10-7 and seemed certain to win.

He looked shell-shocked as van Gerwen was handed the trophy.

"It showed I am so strong at the crucial moment," said van Gerwen later, "and I can come back from any position."

Dennis Priestley v Mike Gregory

1992 BDO World Masters final

THE World Masters was, in Dennis Priestley's opinion, "the second biggest tournament behind the World Championships".

Big in terms of prestige and history – Alan Evans, John Lowe and Eric Bristow were previous winners of a tournament that dated back to 1974 – and numbers.

The BDO reckoned that at the outset of the Masters qualifiers in 1992, there were around one million players competing and by the time the tournament reached the Earls Court Park Inn Hotel in West London, there were 124 left, representing 35 countries.

Priestley and Mike Gregory were the Nos 1 and 2 seeds respectively and lived up to those seedings in matches played over sets that were the best of three legs, rather than the best of five.

Gregory threw the best average of the quarter-finals – an impressive 97.63 in a whitewash of Kevin Spiolek – and in the last four, Priestley pulled off spectacular back-to-back finishes of 136 and 167 to win the deciding set against Alan Warriner and finish the match with an average of 107.13.

Gregory whitewashed Magnus Caris in the other semi-final, meaning Priestley and Gregory would contest their third final of the year.

In both the Swedish Open and Lada Classic finals, Gregory came out on top.

The former went to a deciding 11th leg and Priestley remembered: "I left double eight after nine darts in the last leg – and still lost."

That's how good Gregory could be.

Priestley regarded Gregory as "a dogged competitor".

"He was hard to beat. He just seemed to tighten up when it came to the majors, for some reason. The only thing missing from his CV was a major title."

Gregory had reached the World Masters final before, in 1983, his breakthrough year.

He reached three finals that year – and lost the lot.

Nine years later, Gregory was still reaching finals – and losing them.

He gave darts its very own Devon Loch moment in January 1992 when he did everything apart from find the match-winning double in the World Championship final against Phil Taylor.

Priestley would say darts was all about "bottle and temperament" and it would appear he had rather more of both than Gregory.

Their averages were similar – they could be relied upon to post mid-90s – but in the big moments in the big matches, Gregory twitched – and Priestley didn't.

Priestley won the World Championship in 1991 and when he had his chance 12 months later, Gregory admitted he got "excited", rushed his darts and blew it.

Priestley never did that.

He was the least excitable of throwers.

Regardless of the match situation, he gave every dart the same care and attention, giving his opponents plenty of time to think as he lined up his throw, while Gregory was more fluent and instinctive – and unreliable.

Priestley had the darts in the opening set of the best-of-five-sets final – and was a bit wayward with them. "Oop a bit," he said after his second dart went into the single one.

Gregory won that opening leg – and held to clinch the set.

The second set was closer. It went to a deciding third leg and, with Priestley sitting on 81, Gregory found double top with his last dart for 2-0. Two sets down in a best-of-five-sets match, Priestley nevertheless felt there was no need to panic.

"I didn't do anything wrong," he said, "and I was 2-0 down.

"I missed the odd dart here and there, but not much.

"He just played better than me, but I wasn't playing that badly."

Priestley felt that if Gregory dipped a bit, or he upped it a bit, he could turn the match his way.

But still, he had to start winning legs soon – or the match would be lost.

Priestley upped it in the opening leg of the third set – firing in three successive 140s – and Gregory couldn't go with him.

The next leg was closer. They matched each other dart for dart and there was pressure on Priestley when he sought to check out 25.

Gregory wasn't far behind him on 52, but Priestley's nerve held and two darts later, it was 2-1.

Priestley had to break in the fourth set and though he fashioned a shot at a finish in the first leg, it was at a mighty 161 – and Gregory was well placed on 76 if he missed.

Priestley found treble 20 and treble 17, but was just off target at the bull's-eye, handing Gregory a chance to hold his throw.

He had one dart at double top – and let out a groan after pulling it around an inch below his target.

The rather more composed Priestley mopped up 76 in two darts for a break that changed the course of the match.

Priestley had the darts in the next leg to level at 2-2 – and should the match go to a deciding fifth set, he would have the advantage again.

Priestley made sure of the fourth set by taking out 25 under pressure – Gregory had thrown a maximum 180 to leave four – before the first leg of the fifth set brought another twist.

Priestley couldn't have been any closer to a hold of throw – he bent the wire with a dart at double eight – and Gregory was on the brink after sticking his next dart in double 19.

Gregory was now only a hold away from victory.

Priestley responded with three successive 140s, but missed darts at double 18 and double nine, leaving Gregory a chance at 101 for the match.

He hit treble 20, then single one to leave what commentator Tony Green described as his "favourite double" with his last dart.

That last dart was thrown well enough, but, to Gregory's anguish, it landed on top of the wire, the width of a flight away from the match, the title and £7,000.

Priestley was reprieved, but still had to mop up nine to save the match. He shouted, "Yeaaahh!" in relief after finding double two with his last dart to send the match into a tiebreak.

The set had to be won by two clear legs and again, the third leg was a close one. Priestley left himself 110 to hold, with Gregory on 80.

To finish, Priestley needed a treble – and couldn't find it with his first dart. Single 20 left him 90.

He put his next dart in treble 18, then shifted his sights a couple of inches or so and fired in double 18 for a hold.

"It's Mike's turn to think," Green told viewers before the start of the fourth leg, but he didn't appear to do too much thinking – until he took aim at that favourite double 20 for the leg.

He was too high with his first dart… and his second… and his third.

That gave Priestley a shot at 66 for the match. He had a dart at double 16 – and pushed it just outside the wire.

Gregory had a chance to save the match, but when he needed his aim to be true, his throw was jerky and rushed.

He put his first dart in 20 – and the next two just outside double ten.

Priestley was off target at double 16, but found double eight with his next dart for the match – and wept with joy.

Both posted three-figure averages – Priestley had 102.27, Gregory 100.14 – after what *Darts World* described as "a superb exhibition of determination, skill and accuracy".

Looking back on his career, Priestley regarded the match as "one of my greatest performances".

Phil Taylor v Michael van Gerwen

2013 PDC World Championship final

ALL the talk was about a new era in darts. Phil Taylor was 52 years old and seemed to be tired of the sport, while Michael van Gerwen, just eight months old when Taylor won his first World Championship in 1990, was young, fast, fearless and didn't miss much. Even Taylor himself said before they met in the final of the 2013 PDC World Championship: "I've never seen a player like him before."

In 2006, van Gerwen had come to prominence when, aged just 17 years and 174 days, he became the youngest winner of a major ranking event with victory over Martin Adams in the final of the BDO World Masters. The following year, in about the same time it takes to read this sentence, he threw a nine-darter against Raymond van Barneveld in the Masters of Darts.

Van Gerwen made the switch to the PDC and on his World Championship debut in 2008, he was a double 12 away from beating Taylor in the first round.

Twelve months later, Taylor whitewashed him in the second round.

The 2013 PDC World Championships at Alexandra Palace were made more significant by who wouldn't be there. The voice of darts had been silenced when Sid Waddell, the wild-eyed excitable whose high-brow Geordie screechings made darts watchable to millions, lost his life to cancer in August 2012 and in his memory, the PDC named their World Championship trophy after him.

Nobody was keener to get their hands on the new trophy than Taylor. Waddell had been a friend and Taylor's biggest fan. He had ghostwritten his autobiography *The Power*, and introduced the darts public to the word "incomparable" for Masters of Ceremonies to mispronounce.

Taylor wanted to win the World Championship again for Sid – and for himself. He had been stuck on 15 world titles for two years and Eric Bristow told the press before the start of the tournament: "If Phil doesn't win the World Championship this year, he will never win it again. You can never write Phil off, but not many players have long gaps between winning big titles."

Adrian Lewis headed to Alexandra Palace as the defending champion and although he declared himself "100 per cent confident" of winning the World Championship for the third successive year, he admitted van Gerwen was, on form over the previous six months, the best player in the world.

Van Gerwen had endured a sticky spell – "I was in my own little prison and it felt like there was no way out" – before rebuilding confidence on the PDC Youth circuit.

He returned to claim his first major ranking victory on the PDC Tour – the World Grand Prix in October 2012 – and, despite an inflamed Achilles tendon that meant he spent Christmas Day in hospital, he fired in impressive averages at Alexandra Palace that would have been even more impressive had he been more accurate on his doubles.

He didn't miss much against James Wade in the semi-finals. In the fifth set, van Gerwen fired in a nine-darter and in the next leg, he was millimetres away from another. This time, his dart at double 12 landed the wrong side of the wire and although Wade hit back, the Dutchman still won 6-4.

Taylor's semi-final was more troubled. He had dropped just one set in victories over Mickey Mansell, Jerry Hendriks, Robert Thornton and Andy Hamilton to set up a meeting with Raymond van Barneveld and there were signs of friction between the darts behemoths before the match.

In separate interviews, van Barneveld said he wasn't scared of Taylor; Taylor responded that he should be. What followed Taylor's 6-4 win – van Barneveld came back from 5-1 down to make a match of it – was still unexpected, however. Taylor reacted angrily when van Barneveld grabbed his hand and pulled him towards him to offer his congratulations. Even the most occasional of lip-reading students could tell what Taylor said to van Barneveld as he wriggled himself free of his grip.

"I reacted disgracefully and I feel terrible," said Taylor the following day. "I'd walk away tomorrow if people feel so much animosity towards me. At the moment, I would. I feel very down, very low."

Because of concerns over Taylor's mental state following his semi-final spat and van Gerwen's form, the bookmakers made the Dutchman a 4/5 favourite – the first time Taylor had been a betting underdog since a Premier League match against van Barneveld back in March 2007.

Earlier in the tournament, van Gerwen had said that Taylor was beatable and he had proved it by winning their previous two matches, in the Grand Slam of Darts and Players Championship. But they were over the best of 19 and 11 legs respectively and the World Championship final was over the best of 13 sets, what Taylor would call "a proper game of darts". For all van Gerwen's good form against Taylor recently, the record books showed that of their previous 18 matches, Taylor had won 14.

In the hour before their biggest-ever match, Taylor, appearing in his 19th world final, looked to be handling the pressure better. Van Gerwen solemnly sucked on cigarettes outside the venue's back entrance, while Taylor, despite being troubled by a bout of flu that had dogged him throughout the tournament, chatted cheerfully to well-wishers.

Taylor showed his confidence by handing the throw to the Dutchman after winning the nearest the bull's-eye – and it was a big risk. Throw poorly for a few minutes and van Gerwen would race away.

Taylor didn't throw poorly – he nailed a 170 checkout in the second leg of the match – but still van Gerwen raced away. Taylor found himself 2-0 down after a no-nonsense finish of 98 and mouthed: "What can I do?" to his family and friends in the crowd. He had time to turn things around – the match was the best of 13 sets – and after pegging back the third set, Taylor found inspiration in the fourth from a chant of: "Stand up for Sid Waddell". In a special moment, he responded to a crowd who had given him a mixed reception before the match by throwing a maximum. He then raised a thumb to the heavens. "Sid threw that one for me," he said afterwards.

Taylor went on to win the fourth set to level the match at 2-2, but the next two went to van Gerwen. Taylor knew the seventh set would be crucial. Win it and he would trail only 4-3, but at 5-2 ahead van Gerwen would need only two more sets. "I knew I had to win that set," said Taylor.

Van Gerwen had chances to win the set – and missed them. He was way off target with a dart at double 19 – his dart landed nearer the treble – and he missed double 16 as well.

Darts' new era, Taylor decided, could wait. He won the set to make it 4-3 and had the throw to level the match in the eighth. He took encouragement from a change in the Dutchman's body language.

"Michael was throwing off one leg, his leg was lifting up," said Taylor. "He was throwing his last dart and sometimes it was going in, but a lot of times it was dropping an inch below. He was thinking about being world champion. He looked like he was under pressure and I thought: 'Now's the time to hit him.' That's when I had to hit him as hard as I could."

For a shark like Taylor, those signs were akin to blood in the water – and he pounced. He levelled the match by winning the eighth set, but van Gerwen wasn't finished yet. The ninth set became the sixth of the match to go to a fifth and deciding leg and Taylor handled the pressure better. Van Gerwen couldn't take out 107 and Taylor nailed double top to lead the match for the first time at 5-4.

Taylor held his throw in the tenth set – winning it with an 11-darter – then polished off the match by winning the next with a 91 checkout moments after casually handing out a lozenge to a member of the crowd.

Taylor had won five sets without reply – dropping just five legs – to finish with a three-dart average of 103.04, claim the £200,000 winner's cheque and lift the Sid Waddell Trophy that he handed to the commentator's widow, Irene.

To nobody's surprise, Taylor told the press afterwards: "I'm not going to retire. I'm going to keep pushing on, keep trying to improve.

"Had I not won, it would have been that much more difficult to believe I can win it again.

"I can win more of these titles. Can I win 20? I would because the prize money is going up. It is not about the money, though that is fantastic. Winning is the be-all and end-all."

Steve Coote v Shaun Greatbatch

2002 Dutch Open final

IF there's one thing that annoys Shaun Greatbatch it's that you probably think Phil Taylor threw the first nine-darter shown live on television.

He didn't. Greatbatch did.

"Only proper darts fans know the truth," said Greatbatch.

'Proper darts fans' will probably know there had been televised nine-darters before 2002.

Two of them.

In 1984, John Lowe threw the first in front of the cameras and five-and-a-bit years later, Paul Lim, from the USA via Singapore and Chiswick, threw another at the BDO World Championship.

Neither was shown live on television, however.

Going into the Dutch Open in 2002, Greatbatch had never thrown a nine-darter – "or even come close", he admitted – but knew he had to do something special or his career would be over.

"I didn't have a sponsor and was struggling for money," he said. "I had emptied my savings to pay for the trip and really did think I would have to pack up darts after the tournament."

Had Greatbatch retired, the story would have barely got a mention in his local paper.

Although he had represented England, by his own admission, Greatbatch was struggling on the circuit and was possibly best known for the look on his face when a streaker showed off her charms during his first-round match with Ted Hankey at the 2001 BDO World Championship.

Greatbatch's family were better known.

In the 1950s, his uncle, Trevor Peachey, won the News of the World Individual championship, and parents Sandra and Barry played for England and at Super League level respectively.

"Over in Holland I was a nobody," admitted Greatbatch. "I was unranked and nobody had any idea who I was or what I could do. I had to borrow Mervyn King's VIP pass to make it a bit more comfortable."

King was one of the players people were talking about before the Dutch Open, along with Tony O'Shea, Andy Fordham, Ted Hankey and Raymond van Barneveld, the defending champion and double world champion.

The Dutch Open was a prestigious event.

First held in 1973, a year before the World Masters started, previous winners included Steve Beaton, Hankey and King and the tournament was screened live on Dutch television.

To the surprise of viewers – and everyone else – van Barneveld made an early exit, beaten by Greatbatch's roommate, Steve Coote, and Greatbatch survived a scare against John MaGowan.

"John thought he had beaten me," said Greatbatch. "He took out a finish and turned to shake my hand, but he had miscounted."

Greatbatch made the most of his reprieve, taking out a ton-plus finish to win the match, and he added the scalp of Co Stompe on his way to the final, where he met Coote.

"Out of 2,613 players there I ended up playing my roommate in the final," said Greatbatch.

"Steve was ranked in the top 16 at the time, but I thought: 'This is here for the taking. It's down to me.' I knew that if I kept myself together and played as well as I had been doing I could push him all the way."

Greatbatch had built plenty of momentum. The final was his seventh match of the day, his "12th or 13th" of the weekend, and he said: "When you play all day you get into a groove and the game becomes easier. But it's the same for everyone else. They all play better as well."

Nobody ever threw nine better darts than Greatbatch…

The opening set of the best-of-seven-sets final went to Coote – and Greatbatch hit back to grab the opening two legs of the second.

Throwing to save the set, Coote started the third leg with 96 and Greatbatch's first three darts landed within a millimetre or two of each other – in the treble 20.

"If your first dart is good," explained Greatbatch, "you can usually follow it."

His fourth, fifth and sixth darts landed in the same place as his first three darts, give or take a millimetre or two.

The nine-dart leg was on.

"I threw the back-to-back 180s and thought that was the hard bit done," said Greatbatch. "I knew it was a great chance. I just had to let go of the last three darts right…"

Greatbatch wasn't clever enough to blow his chance.

"Some people are too intelligent to play darts," he said. "If you think too much and do too much worrying you're never going to make a darts player.

"Most top darts players don't have too much between their ears and it definitely helps.

"I'm not exactly Einstein myself!"

Einstein would have figured out there are several ways to take out 141 with three darts – even if he couldn't do it himself – and Greatbatch chose the treble 20, treble 15, double 18 route.

His seventh, eighth and ninth darts all found the middle of their targets.

Shaun shook his fists in celebration – and the crowd thundered their approval.

"It was perfect," he said of the most perfect of perfect legs.

"All the darts were in the middle. I had never thrown darts like it before and I haven't thrown darts like it since either.

"When I threw the nine-darter, Steve [Coote] was as happy as I was and whenever I speak to him now he always calls me the bloke who made him famous."

History had been made, but for Greatbatch, there was still a match to be won.

"You see players throw nine-darters – and still lose the match," he said. I didn't want to lose the game. It would have been my first major win and I knew it would kick-start my career.

"After the nine-darter I just wanted to calm down and get the match won, but the next three darts I threw were 41 – and the crowd cheered just as loudly as they had when I threw the nine-darter."

Greatbatch regrouped well enough to win the match – and a first prize of €2,500 that he was so busy spending, he missed his flight home. "Mervyn had to give me a lift to the ferry," he said.

Although the Dutch Open offered no prize for a nine-dart leg, a darts-mad businessman was impressed enough to hand Greatbatch a €2,000 bonus – and there was the promise of much more.

"I had sponsors coming out of my ears after that," said Greatbatch. "Those nine darts saved my career and from there I shouldn't have looked back."

Later that year, Greatbatch missed a double for another nine-darter in Germany, he reached the semi-finals of the BDO World Championships in 2006 and by the summer of 2008, he had climbed up to No. 5 in the BDO world rankings.

He was robbed of his chance to climb higher.

Greatbatch was diagnosed with bone marrow cancer and by the time he toed the oche at the Lakeside Country Club the following January, his hair had fallen out and he had lost four inches in height.

Happily, Greatbatch's health recovered – but there would be no return to competitive darts.

"When I was No. 5 in the world I was bashing people up and felt so confident," he said, "I thought I could beat anyone.

"I was going to join the PDC and I'm fairly sure I would have made a good living out of darts.

"But by the time I had recovered from my illness the fire had gone. I knew I was going to have to start all over again and I just thought: 'What's the point?'

"Lying in hospital for six weeks makes you think and I decided to do other things.

"Darts was my life and I want to do other things now. I do some match fishing and go to watch Norwich City."

To celebrate the tenth anniversary of his perfect leg, Greatbatch was invited back to the Dutch Open in 2012.

"They showed the nine-darter on the big screen and the crowd behaved as though it was the first time they had seen it," he said. "They all went mental when the last dart went in. It made me cry.

"People who live next door to me don't know who I am, but I can't go anywhere in Holland without people asking for autographs and photographs.

"Whenever I was at the airport, people would always shout 'Nine-dart!' when they saw me."

Paul Lim v Jack McKenna

1990 BDO World Championship second round

PAUL Lim always fancied his chances of throwing a nine-darter.

"I used to think: 'I have hit 180s and finished 141 many times,'" he said, "and if I put that together in one game, there is the nine-darter.

"It sounds easy enough…"

It wasn't.

After more than a decade of regular televised darts, only John Lowe, at the less than salubrious Fulcrum Centre in Slough in October 1984, had achieved darts perfection and the wait for a nine-darter at 'the Embassy', otherwise known as the BDO World Championship, went on.

Jocky Wilson and Bob Anderson had come close.

Wilson wired double 18 in 1983 and when Anderson fashioned a shot six years later, he was off target at double 12 by what he says was "a considerable margin".

"The nine-darter was like a myth," said Lim. "It seemed so hard."

Lim added to the myth himself when, during his first-round match against Ray Battye in 1990, he threw six perfect darts, then fluffed his lines.

Lim went on to win 3-2, setting up a second-round match against Jack McKenna, who had upset Peter Evison in the first round.

McKenna was a phlegmatic veteran from the Republic of Ireland, while the well-travelled Lim represented Singapore, Papua New Guinea, the USA – and West London!

Lim remembers that, growing up in Singapore, there was a rubber ring nailed to the back of the toilet door at the family home and for hour after hour, he and his uncle would try to throw "little plastic darts with a steel point" into the middle of it.

That gave him a feel for darts and at 21 years old, he started throwing them at a board at the Robin Hood pub in Chiswick, near the house he was sharing with a group of fellow trainee chefs.

The housemates chipped in with 50 pence each to buy the winner's prize for their novice darts competition, a bottle of whisky.

Lim won, but, because he didn't drink, he gave away his winnings. "My friends were glad they lost," he laughed.

Lim decided to invest in a set of darts, started to play more regularly and though he says he "won most tournaments on the USA circuit", when he ventured to Britain, he suffered defeats that left him believing he couldn't compete at the highest level.

"I had no confidence," remembered Lim.

That changed after he met Tony Jenkins, who played county darts for Surrey.

"We met through a mutual friend and Tony asked to practise with me to get ready for the LA Open and North American Open," remembered Lim.

"I was beating him up on the board and after a few days, he told me: 'Paul, with the way you are playing, you should not have any problem competing on the UK circuit.'

"After he said that, I started to play with so much confidence. I won the LA Open singles and doubles and beat a lot of good British players."

Lim remembers what he describes as a breakthrough win over Bob Anderson and he went on to establish himself as a solid top-16 player.

"I was never a Taylor or a Bristow," admitted Lim, but, on his day, he was a handful for anyone.

Lim had a good 1989.

He was climbing towards the top ten in the rankings heading into the World Championships, where his record was poor.

"Horrible!" was how he described it.

The 35-year-old had played at the Lakeside eight times – and had yet to get beyond the second round.

He reached the second round in 1990 with that win over Battye, a Yorkshireman who was sliding down the rankings after peaking at No. 8, and McKenna was next.

McKenna had reached the WDF World Cup final a few months earlier, losing to Bristow, but really, this was considered a match between fringe contenders for the World Championship.

There was no live coverage on television, only late-night high-lights on the BBC.

The directors didn't bother with the first set of Lim–McKenna, won by Lim, and skipped to the start of the second.

McKenna threw 100 – and Lim answered with 180.

"Any player that says they don't think about a nine-darter after starting a leg with 180 is the biggest liar ever!" he joked.

"But I wasn't nervous. I was in the zone that all darts players long for. It seems so easy when you are in that zone. I didn't slow down, I didn't stop and think. I felt in control."

Lim didn't notice McKenna's throw of 134 and, to increasingly excited cries of: "Yes!" from commentator Tony Green, put his next three darts in the treble 20.

The nine-darter was on.

The shouts of: "Gwaaaan Paul!" were hushed as he took aim and with three apparently effortless flicks of his wrist that sent darts into treble 20, treble 19 and double 12, Lim became a darts immortal – and £52,000 richer.

"It's happened at last, here at the World Championship!" cried Green.

"The crowd are happy and with £52,000 in the bank, so is he!"

So was the referee, the late Martin Fitzmaurice.

He remembered: "You have little room to manoeuvre up there [on stage], and when he hit the final treble 20, it covered double 12, so I couldn't see it directly.

"I was hoping he didn't hit 57, then double 12, but he went and hit 57.

"There was no way in the world, with £52,000 riding on one dart, that I was going to move.

"So he threw it, the crowd went into bedlam, and I called: 'Game, shot...'

"It was only then that I checked it was in.

"At two o'clock in the morning, I woke up in a cold sweat, thinking: 'What if it hadn't gone in?'"

For Lim, the nine-darter made the rest of the match – and tournament – more difficult.

"After the nine-darter, it was really hard to concentrate and I was lucky to go through," he said. "The nine-darter really got in my head and every game I played after that, I could hear the audience chanting: 'Nine-darter! Nine-darter!'"

More than a quarter of a century on, Lim, who bowed out in the quarter-finals to Cliff Lazarenko, still hears it.

"Wherever I go," he said, "they all remember the nine-darter. I have won many tournaments, but I will always treasure that nine-darter as the No. 1 moment in my darts career."

Trina Gulliver v Anastasia Dobromyslova

2008 BDO Women's World Championship
final

THERE seemed to be three certainties in life – death, taxes and Trina Gulliver winning the BDO Women's World Championship.

Make that four certainties. Gulliver always beats Francis Hoenselaar in the final.

The BDO introduced the Women's Championship in 2001 and for the next seven years Gulliver lifted the trophy, often recording averages that compared favourably with the men who, as she was quick to point out, earned much greater rewards for their talents.

On her way to winning the title in 2007, Gulliver beat a 22-year-old from Russia in the semi-finals.

Anastasia Dobromyslova was born in Tver, around 100 miles from Moscow, and as an 11-year-old, she was intrigued by an after-school club that advertised judo, table tennis... and darts.

By then, Dobromyslova had decided ice skating, roller skating, basketball and volleyball weren't really for her, but found darts was more to her liking.

She went on to win six Russian titles, but admits the competition could have been tougher.

"Hardly anyone in Russia plays darts," she said.

Outside her home country, Dobromyslova won the Girls' title at the BDO World Masters in 2001 and had a breakthrough win over Gulliver in the Dutch Open in 2004.

The following year, she met Tony Martin, a professional darter himself, and they became an item.

Martin found the BDO circuit a struggle, but had good news for his other half towards the end of 2006.

Dobromyslova remembered: "I won a tournament – the British Open – and my boyfriend said: 'You're going to the Lakeside!' I just said: 'Okaaay...' I didn't know I was that close to qualifying."

Dobromyslova was a winner on her Lakeside debut in January 2007, whitewashing Carina Ekberg in the last eight, and had her chances in her semi-final against defending champion Gulliver, but missed them and lost 2-0.

Commentators were puzzled by some of her shot selections during the match and when asked about it afterwards, Dobromyslova explained she struggled to aim at certain parts of the board because she felt her feet were "stuck" to the oche through nerves.

The defeat didn't dent Dobromyslova, it drove her on.

"Whenever I lose in a tournament, I get angry and upset and put in a few extra hours in practice," she said.

Dobromyslova returned to the Lakeside 12 months later having "put in a few extra hours" and determined to do herself justice.

She threw what commentator David Croft described as "elegant and clinical" darts in whitewashes of Dee Bateman and Stephanie Smee and when asked whether she had any fear of the defending champion she would meet in the final, Dobromyslova shook her head emphatically.

Gulliver, taken to a deciding leg by Hoenselaar in the previous year's final, dropped a set in her quarter-final against Julie Gore before coming through 2-1 and rather pummelled Karin Krappen in the semi-finals.

She took that form with her into the final, starting with 180 to put Dobromyslova under pressure immediately.

Given the way Dobromyslova had folded when she met Gulliver in the semi-finals 12 months earlier, she could have fallen apart, but this time, Dobromyslova held her game together and took the opening set to a deciding fifth leg.

Gulliver had the darts, but as was sometimes her problem, she blocked the treble 20 with them.

Dobromyslova chipped away with three tons, then flung in 165.

That left 36 after 12 darts and Gulliver, so dominant at the Lakeside for so long, needed Dobromyslova to miss six times if she was going to have any chance of holding her throw and winning the set. Dobromyslova missed a couple of times – her first dart veered into double four – but found double 14 with her third dart and the set was hers.

Gulliver had been behind in finals before, but this time, she had lost a set against the darts. She had to break back in the second set – or the match was lost.

Both threw 140s in the opening leg of the second set as they duelled for control and Dobromyslova left herself 90 with Gulliver on 96.

Dobromyslova went for treble 20 and hit the single, then did it again, leaving the bull's-eye.

No problem.

"Well done," said Gulliver sportingly as her World Championship slipped away.

Dobromyslova could see the finish line now and pushed for a break of throw in the second leg. Her first maximum 180 of the match left her 81 with Gulliver way back on 303.

Again, Dobromyslova had six darts to find the finishing double – and this time, she needed only one.

That left her throwing for the match and she started the leg confidently with 140.

Gulliver could only respond with scores of 41 and 11. She really needed a big score to drag herself back into the leg – and for a split second, she had it.

Gulliver put two darts in the treble 20, but her third knocked the other two out, leaving her with a score of 60 rather than 180.

"I knew then it wasn't going to be my night," she admitted afterwards, but she recovered well enough – and Dobromyslova missed enough – to still get a shot at 72 to save the match.

A wayward first dart – Gulliver aimed for 20 and smiled ruefully when she hit five – meant she only got a dart at the bull's-eye – and was a couple of centimetres away.

Dobromyslova, who had previously missed double 17 and double four for the title, slotted in double two and the World Championship was hers.

She rather stumbled and giggled through the post-match interview, but the smile on her face spoke for itself.

James Wade v Scott Waites

WHO'S the best? PDC or BDO?

The idea of the Grand Slam of Darts was to bring them together to settle the argument.

Instead, it started an argument.

Martin Adams refused his invitation, declaring his loyalty to the BDO, and PDC chairman Barry Hearn said that showed Adams lacked ambition, that he couldn't handle a circuit that was "a hard grind for winners".

The name-calling went on. Adams said the PDC was "a circus", Hearn responded that the BDO was "Mickey Mouse... amateur darts."

Scott Waites would rather not get involved in all that.

A straightforward Yorkshireman, his job as a joiner paid the bills and he threw darts for fun.

"I love playing darts whether it's with my mates at the local or going around the circuit," he said.

"People take darts too seriously. If they enjoyed it more, they would probably play better."

Waites had been successful on the BDO circuit in 2010, winning both the Turkish and Czech Opens in the months before the Grand Slam of Darts at Wolverhampton Civic Hall.

In front of the cameras and the bigger audiences, he usually struggled. Missed doubles cost him in nine-set nail-biters against Darryl Fitton and Martin Phillips in the quarter-finals of the BDO World Championships and he admitted: "The hardest part is blanking out the crowd, the cameras, everything that's going on around you and just concentrating."

Waites held himself together to reach the final of the Grand Slam of Darts in 2009, then fell apart and was thrashed 16-2 by Phil Taylor.

Twelve months later, he was given no chance.

"All my mates went to the bookmakers to look at my odds before the tournament and I was 80/1," said Waites.

"Even though I reached the final the year before, they had completely written me off before I had even thrown a dart.

"I just laughed. Everyone thinks the PDC are so much better than the BDO.

"I think I'm quite a consistent player. I average around 90. On a good day, it goes up to 100, but on a bad day it doesn't drop much below 90."

As always, Taylor was the favourite having lifted the trophy for the previous three years, but James Wade's form was also impressive.

The previous month, he had won the World Grand Prix in Dublin, meaning the World Championship was the only major PDC ranking event missing from his CV.

Wade hadn't won the Grand Slam of Darts either and Taylor's quarter-final exit against Steve Beaton increased his chances.

Wade was very different to the only player above him in the PDC.

He told reporters he didn't enjoy darts and didn't practise much, but with a few vodkas inside him to wash away his demons, Wade could even stay with Taylor – just about.

Taylor threw two nine-darters at him in the 2010 Premier League final – and still only won 10-8.

Even when he was throwing well, Wade still seemed itchy in his own skin. Never did a darts player look so awkward in celebration. He would shrug his shoulders, wiggle his hips, raise his eyebrows…

He could be a difficult, uninterested interviewee and to the 50 or so who made their feelings known on the Facebook page "We Hate James Wade the Dart Player", he was "cocky" and worse.

They willed on whomever he played and in the final of the Grand Slam of Darts in 2010, they willed on Waites.

Of the seven BDO players, only Waites and Ted Hankey made it beyond the group stages.

Hankey was beaten in the second round by Steve Beaton and Waites knocked out Raymond van Barneveld, Co Stompe, then Beaton to reach the final.

"Scott wasn't intimidated by playing the big names," said John Rawling, who commentated on the tournament for ITV. "He believed in himself."

Had it been a drinking contest between Waites and Wade, there was only one winner.

Waites had four cans of Budweiser to take the edge off his pre-match nerves; Wade had much more.

His poison was vodka, lots of it.

Waites started each of the opening three legs with 180, but every maximum was followed by 60, allowing Wade to stay in touch and he found finishes of 107 and 110 – his 15th and 16th ton-plus checkouts in the tournament – within his range to pull away.

Waites puffed out his cheeks and told himself to keep going, but after Wade went 7-0 up, he wasn't thinking about winning any more.

"I was thinking: 'I got two legs last year, let's get three legs this time,'" said Waites. A slither of hope came in the eighth leg.

Although Wade still won it to lead 8-0, it took him 18 darts and over the next five legs, his average dropped by more than ten points, allowing Waites back into the match.

Waites raised his arms in mock celebration to ironic cheers after double 12 gave him the ninth leg – there would be no whitewash – and although at 8-5 there was still work to be done, the momentum was with him.

"I started to think I had a chance," he said.

"I turned round to where my family and friends were sitting, saw my dad wearing a Mickey Mouse T-shirt and thought: 'Just keep calm and play.'

"I just had to keep playing one leg at a time and keep taking my chances.

"When I had one dart at a double, I hit it nearly every time – and James was missing his one dart at a double. That was how the game turned around."

Waites clawed it back to 9-8 and going into the 18th leg, had won eight of the previous nine.

Rather than fall apart, Wade was switched on by the crisis and started to throw his best darts again. He held his throw to lead 10-8, then broke in the next with a 97 checkout.

Wade was a double away from a 12-8 lead, missed three times and the seesaw match swung back Waites' way again.

He went on to level the match at 11-11 with a 121 checkout, then won a scruffy 23rd leg – Waites bust his score, Wade missed three at a double – to lead the match for the first time.

The momentum with him, Waites pulled away to lead 14-11.

Wade held his throw in the 26th leg, but Waites held his nerve, throwing maximums in each of the next two legs to get to the double first and the match-winning double eight sent him jumping around the stage shaking his fists.

Wade shook his head in disbelief.

"I just dug in, gritted my teeth and played darts," said Waites afterwards. "James gave me so many chances, I took my chances and the next thing I knew I was level, then in front.

"I proved everybody completely wrong."

Wade tried to put on a brave face when interviewed by ITV – but couldn't.

"I feel absolutely horrific," he mumbled.

Waites headed to a nearby Irish bar to celebrate into the early hours and weeks later, Wade checked himself into The Priory clinic crippled by depression following his shock second-round defeat to Mensur Suljovic in the World Championships.

"Whenever I see James, he tells me: 'You helped put me in The Priory,'" said Waites.

Aileen de Graaf v Lisa Ashton

2014 BDO Women's World Championship first round

AS a girl growing up in Bolton, Lisa Ashton enjoyed playing most sports – apart from darts.

On the insistence of her four older brothers, she played it anyway.

"They made me do it," she said, "and as I got into it, I got good at it. By the time I was about 16 they stopped asking me to play because I was beating them.

"That's when I realised I could play."

Ashton went on to play darts at the pub, in the Super League for the successful Swinton team, then for her county, Lancashire, her country and at the Lakeside Country Club in the BDO World Championship.

She made her debut there in 2009 – losing to Trina Gulliver in her first match – and in 2013, she threw some wonderfully fast, fluent darts on the way to the final, where she lost to Anastasia Dobromyslova.

The following year, there were 16 entries in the Women's World Championship for the first time – rather than eight as there had been since the tournament started in 2001 – and Ashton was paired with Lakeside debutant Aileen de Graaf in the first round.

At 23, de Graaf, a nurse from Spakenburg, a small village near Utrecht, was seeded No. 7 after a good year – Ashton, 20 years her senior, was unseeded – and had the look of a rising star of the women's sport.

Encouraged to play darts in her teens by her future husband, de Graaf's CV already showed victories at the Zuiderduin Masters, along with the Welsh and Danish Opens and she had also reached the semi-finals of the World Masters.

De Graaf had also beaten Ashton three months before the World Championships, in the quarter-finals of the Tops of Ghent tournament, by a 4-2 scoreline.

She made a confident start to their match at the Lakeside as well, putting her first three darts of the match in the treble 20, and though Ashton replied with a maximum of her own later in the leg, the Dutch thrower held.

'The Rose of Lancashire' – 'The Whirlwind' would also fit, such was the pace of Ashton's game – also held, but after carving out a chance to break in the third leg, she missed. Seven times she missed and from nowhere, de Graaf came back to hold.

Ashton started the fourth leg with 28, de Graaf flung in another maximum and a set that was apparently in Ashton's grasp a few throws earlier was now running away from her.

De Graaf didn't miss her chance. She went on to wrap up the opening set and the cameras zoomed in on Ashton's daughters Danielle and Lindsey, good players themselves, looking concerned.

Ashton had the throw in the second set and again, she couldn't find her doubles.

She missed two at double 16 and three more at double eight, but fortunately for her, de Graaf, so good on her doubles during the first set when she averaged around 90, couldn't hit hers either.

Finally, Ashton found double eight – and it looked like a turning point.

As she occasionally does, Ashton put together an unplayable purple patch when she put her darts wherever she wanted without even appearing to take aim.

"Lisa has a feel for darts," was how Deta Hedman explained it.

Ashton broke in the second leg after taking out 217 in five darts – 137 left her 80 – and wrapped up the set with a breezy 85 checkout, again needing only one dart to find the double after de Graaf had a bounce-out to pull a leg back.

The opening leg of the third set also went Ashton's way, against the darts, after a throw of 177 left her six darts to take out 69.

But just when it seemed Ashton had control of the match, de Graaf fought back, taking out 78 in two darts for a break, with Ashton only a double 18 away from a 2-0 lead in the deciding set.

Ashton found a response and for a third successive leg, there was a break of throw. She took out 104 – the highest checkout of the match – to win the leg and again found her extra gear to press home the advantage. In that no-nonsense way of hers, Ashton put her first four darts of the next leg in the treble 20 to take charge of a leg she needed to win the match.

But as is often the way, she found the match-winning double the hardest to find.

Seven times Ashton missed and de Graaf found her favourite double eight – but only just – with her last dart to force a do-or-die tiebreak leg to decide this high-quality, seesaw match.

Ashton won the nearest the bull's-eye to get the advantage of the throw and after six darts each there were only two points between them.

Ashton was on 282, de Graaf on 284.

Ashton threw 140 and this time, de Graaf couldn't stay with her, scoring just 82.

That left Ashton six darts to take out 142. After four darts, she was on double top for the match.

She missed twice, but got another shot after de Graaf took 100 off 142, a score that guaranteed her two darts at a double – should Ashton miss again.

She missed double 20 to leave double ten, put her next dart in the neighbouring double six and nervelessly tossed her last into double four for the match.

Bobby George described what he had seen as the best women's darts match ever and Ashton provided plenty more drama on the way to lifting the trophy.

She was taken to a deciding fifth set by Tamara Schuur, conqueror of Gulliver, in the last eight, survived six match darts against No. 3 seed Dobromyslova in the semi-finals to scrape through and in the final, Ashton overturned a 2-0 deficit against Hedman to win 3-2.

Simon Whitlock v
Andy Hamilton

2011 World Matchplay quarter-final

IN another book about the worst darts matches, there's a chapter about a match between Andy Hamilton and Mick McGowan.

In their first-round match at the World Matchplay in 2007, Hamilton averaged a woeful 79.63 – and fortunately for him, McGowan was even worse.

He managed just 73.58 – and Hamilton went through 10-6.

Those figures were out of character for Hamilton, a robust, plastic-hammer-wielding Henry VIII lookalike who reached the quarter-finals of the PDC World Championship at the first attempt in 2005 and had been there or thereabouts at just about every major tournament since.

Every pub darts player in Stoke-on-Trent had known all about the Hamiltons for years.

There was James, better known as 'Big Jim', then there were his sons Darren and Andy.

Then there wasn't Andy.

Good enough at 18 years old to play for Cheshire, his priorities changed after he became a father.

"The money wasn't there for me to play county darts," said Hamilton, "and I never had the transport to get to games.

"I fell out of love with the game. I started playing again for fun, but I never really had that competitive streak."

Until several years later when the qualifiers for the 2004 UK Open came to his local.

Hamilton won, went on to reach the televised stages and decided to join the PDC circuit.

At the first attempt, he reached the last eight of the World Championships in 2005, and two years later he was a semi-finalist at the Circus Tavern and reached the final of the Grand Slam of Darts.

Each time he was beaten by Taylor, who likened Hamilton to John Lowe; a steady grafter who was guaranteed to hit a treble every visit and never knew when he was beaten.

But for all his ruddy-cheeked resilience, Hamilton had slipped out of the world's top 16 by the time the 2011 World Matchplay got under way and his first-round draw wasn't kind.

Gary Anderson had won the Premier League a couple of months earlier, and in a shock, Hamilton beat him 10-6, then dug deep again to put out blubbery Scot John Henderson by a 13-11 scoreline.

That set up a quarter-final against Simon Whitlock, known as "the beard to be feared" by Sid Waddell.

In 2008, Whitlock, an intense, wristy thrower, became the first Australian to reach the BDO World Championship final since Tony David six years earlier.

He was beaten 7-5 by top seed Mark Webster and the following year joined the PDC.

In 2010, Whitlock scalped five seeds on his way to reaching the PDC World Championship final and though beaten 7-3 by Phil Taylor, he ended the tournament having thrown a record 58 maximum 180s.

Later that year, Whitlock reached the semi-finals at the World Matchplay, and the following year he headed to Blackpool as the No. 5 seed and wins over Peter Wright (10-7) and Denis Ovens (13-1) put him through to the quarter-finals.

Whitlock went 4-1 up, Hamilton stayed in touch at 6-4, but Whitlock won six of the next seven legs for 12-5.

He stayed in control and at 15-8, Whitlock was just a leg away from the match.

Hamilton would later admit he was "trying to pinch a leg here or there" to make the scoreline more respectable, but discovered: "When I started feeling I had nothing to lose, the 180s started flying in."

Hamilton held for 15-9, then broke in the next with the help of his seventh and eighth maximums of the match.

Commentator Stuart Pyke still reckoned Hamilton "needed a miracle".

For the miracle to happen, Hamilton would have to up his average by around ten points and Whitlock would have to start missing.

In the 26th leg, Whitlock started missing.

He was some way off with three darts at double top for the match and with his last, do-or-die dart, Hamilton fired in double 16 to finish off an 86 checkout for 15-11.

Hamilton held in the next and would later admit: "When I got to 12 legs I thought: 'I can win this.'"

The crowd shared his belief.

They chanted "In-ger-lund and "There's only one Andy Hamilton" and willed him on.

Hamilton, accepting of defeat a few minutes earlier, now sensed victory was possible, and would later say the crowd's backing "gave me an extra five per cent.

"I think Simon had got so far ahead that he lost concentration and forgot he still had to win the match."

If Whitlock had been comfortable, feeling the match-winning chances would keep coming and that eventually he would take one, he surely wasn't feeling so certain of that at 15-12.

As often happens in darts matches, he had discovered the match-winning double was the hardest to find, but though Whitlock was struggling, he was still only 12 or 15 well-directed darts away from victory.

The 28th leg was another nail-biter. With Whitlock sitting on 36 for the match, Hamilton found double five with his last dart for 15-13.

Whitlock missed another chance to win the match in the next leg – his fourth in total – and as he went to pick his dart out of the board, he struggled to conceal a rueful grin.

Maybe Whitlock was starting to think it wasn't going to be his day…

"You can sense how the other player's feeling," said Hamilton. "You can read their body language.

"When they're looking at their feet instead of standing there with their chest out, you can tell they are feeling the pressure and that gives you confidence."

As the crowd chanted his name, Hamilton found double 16 with his first dart for 15-14, then held to send the match into a tiebreak.

Whitlock had the throw in the 31st leg, got to the double first, missed it and kept missing.

He spurned five chances to take the leg and after six missed doubles of his own, Hamilton was able to correct his radar and find double four.

At 16-15, Hamilton led for the first time and a hold of throw in the 32nd leg would win him the match.

Again, Whitlock had his chances – and missed them. He put two darts wide of double 18, but with Hamilton on 94, there was a chance Whitlock would be back to try for double 18 again.

Hamilton went for the bull's-eye, hit 25 and 19 with his next dart left the bull's-eye. For the match. With his last dart.

He stepped across the oche, took aim and threw …

"IN-CRE-DI-BULL!" screamed Pyke after Hamilton added an exclamation mark to what co-commentator John Gwynne described as "the greatest comeback ever in the World Matchplay and maybe in professional darts anywhere."

In the space of a breathless 32 minutes, Hamilton had turned certain defeat into victory.

Six months later, he did it again.

Hamilton and Whitlock met in the semi-finals of the PDC World Championship at Alexandra Palace and from 5-3 down, Hamilton clawed his way back to win an epic, two-and-a-half-hour battle of wills in an 11th-set tiebreak.

Though that win took Hamilton through to his first World Championship final – where he was beaten by Adrian Lewis – he would rather remember his great escape in Blackpool.

"The format in the World Championship [matches are played over sets rather than legs] means I could afford to lose a few legs and still win the match," said Hamilton.

"But I had to win every leg in Blackpool. I really had to dig in and show what I'm made of. That's why it's my favourite match."

One of mine too…

Phil Taylor v
Raymond van Barneveld

2006 Premier League, week five,
Bournemouth

RAYMOND van Barneveld had won four BDO World Championships – and it wasn't enough.

"People would tell me: 'You've won so many titles in the BDO, but there is a guy playing in another organisation and we think he is better than you,'" he said.

Phil Taylor was, in the words of commentator Sid Waddell, "the greatest darts player who ever drew breath" and there was no disputing that. He had won 13 world titles and to prove he was better than him, van Barneveld would have to join the PDC.

For months, he wondered what to do.

"I could have stayed with the BDO," he said, "but I told myself that when I look back, I don't want to think that I never had the balls to play the best players in the world.

"But I was still not sure. I wanted to equal Bristow's record by winning a fifth BDO world title."

Bristow taunted van Barneveld in a newspaper interview before the start of the 2006 BDO World Championship, saying he was "frightened" to join the PDC and play Taylor.

But it wasn't Bristow's goading or the loss to Jelle Klaasen in the final that made up van Barneveld's mind.

It was a night in front of the television…

Klaasen was shown celebrating in his world title success with well-wishers at his local pub.

"The crowd were chanting: 'Jelle! Jelle!'" remembered van Barneveld, "and then they started singing: 'Who the fuck is Barney?'

"That's when I made my decision.

"The BDO is big in Holland and I felt loyalty to them, but when I heard that I knew they didn't deserve me any more.

"There were a lot of people sitting in my living room when that came on television and I told them: 'I want to join the PDC.' Even [wife] Sylvia was open-mouthed. It was a big shock to people in Holland.

"People have short memories. They forget what I have done for the sport in Holland."

Five million viewers – that's a third of the population – had tuned in to watch van Barneveld win his first BDO World Championship in 1998 and there were Beatlemaniaesque scenes at Schiphol Airport when he returned home.

It didn't last. By the time he joined the PDC, van Barneveld said Dutch fans always cheered for his opponent and he never did understand why.

Across the North Sea, van Barneveld's marksmanship was better appreciated and when it was revealed he had accepted a wild card invitation into the PDC Premier League, the news was well received – especially by Taylor. He was full of praise for van Barneveld, but how much of a threat was he?

From 1994, they threw on opposite sides of the darts divide, but still met each other at open events in Canada and Switzerland and tournaments such as the World Darts Gala in Holland.

And Taylor usually won.

Before van Barneveld joined the PDC, Taylor had won nine of their 11 matches – including the one-hour challenge at Wembley Arena in 1999 that brought together the rival world champions.

Van Barneveld's first victory over Taylor came at the fourth attempt in the Swiss Open in 2000 – and he said it was the turning point of his career.

"I was crying after that game," he said. "It was such a big victory for me. I had been thinking I couldn't beat him.

"That was the most important match of my life. When you have beaten the best player in the world, your mindset changes."

The challenge now was to beat him regularly on the sport's biggest stage and over the previous decade or so, every attempt to topple Taylor had failed. Dennis Priestley and John Part had their occasional successes, but ultimately, Taylor saw them all off.

He had raised the bar beyond everyone else's reach. Taylor would give away the advantage of the throw and still win, usually with a three-figure average, and to keep him motivated the ever-expanding PDC came up with new trophies to win, like the Premier League.

Taylor won the inaugural Premier League in 2005 and 12 months later, van Barneveld, Colin Lloyd, Peter Manley, Wayne Mardle, Roland Scholten and Ronnie Baxter tried to take the trophy off him.

The seven players would meet each other twice at venues across the country on Thursday nights and after 12 weeks, the top four in the table qualified for the semi-finals.

Hundreds had seen Taylor win the inaugural Premier League – and thousands saw him defend it as bigger venues were booked to satisfy demand for tickets.

Leaving the BDO was a bold move appreciated by the King George's Hall crowd in Blackburn and van Barneveld was cheered loudly before, during and after his 8-1 walloping of Baxter.

But when van Barneveld said in a moody Sky Sports advertisement that he "joined the PDC for one man", he didn't mean Baxter.

The man he came to play was Taylor, and four weeks later they met in Bournemouth.

Not since 'The Match of the Century' seven years earlier had Taylor and van Barneveld played each other in Britain and if fans and pundits were already excited at the prospect, they were even more excited after van Barneveld opened the night by throwing a nine-darter in his 8-3 thumping of Manley.

Now for Taylor . . .

The theory went, Taylor was vulnerable in shorter matches, but despite that, he hadn't dropped a point in the competition since he drew with Wayne Mardle on the opening night.

The best-of-14-legs format in the Premier League meant a draw was possible, but van Barneveld was in Bournemouth to win.

He threw fearlessly against Taylor, broke in the third leg and opened up a 3-1 lead.

Taylor pegged it back to 3-3 with finishes of 120 and 95 and at 4-4, the match was in the balance.

Taylor then upped a gear. He won the ninth leg in 12 darts with van Barneveld way back on 279, broke in the next and added the 11th leg to lead 7-4 and secure at least a draw.

At that point, van Barneveld couldn't win the match; perhaps he would never beat Taylor. Neither Roland Scholten nor Colin Lloyd had ever beaten him in a major televised event...

With the game almost lost, van Barneveld counter-attacked.

He held his throw in the 12th leg after Taylor cranked up the pressure by starting with back-to-back 140s, then broke in 11 darts to set up a deciding 14th leg.

Van Barneveld had to hold his throw to pick up a point and having been 7-4 behind, a draw would seem like a victory.

Taylor wouldn't settle for a draw, he simply had to win, but there was plenty of fight in van Barneveld as well.

In van Barneveld, Taylor met an adversary who felt the pain of defeat as deeply as him and who would give his all to avoid that anguish. So for the next few minutes, van Barneveld and Taylor threw everything at each other in one of darts' greatest-ever legs.

Van Barneveld started with back-to-back 140s, then 41, Taylor responded with 140, 141 and 140.

That left him 80 and with van Barneveld sitting on 40 after his third 140 of the leg, Taylor had to take it out with his next three darts.

But he missed a dart at double top for the match – and so did van Barneveld.

He missed double ten as well and had to be on target with his last dart or he was sure to lose. Van Barneveld didn't think about any of that, shut out the crowd who whooped, screamed and shrieked, and matter-of-factly stuck his last dart in double ten. The match was saved.

Clearly this wasn't the same van Barneveld who had unravelled against Taylor so many times before. Taylor would not have things all his own way against him any more.

A new rivalry was born…

Michael van Gerwen v Peter Wright

2015 World Series of Darts final

IN 2015, Michael van Gerwen was winning everything.

He won The Masters, UK Open and World Matchplay and in the space of three weeks, the 26-year-old Dutchman added the European Championship and the Grand Slam of Darts, throwing possibly the most exhilarating darts ever seen.

Victory at the latter event in Wolverhampton – where BDO stalwart Martin 'Wolfie' Adams was a popular entrant – meant van Gerwen had won all the major tournaments on the PDC circuit during his career.

In the Grand Slam semi-finals, he beat Phil Taylor, who confessed afterwards that van Gerwen "got his back up" with his gurning, fist-shaking celebrations.

Van Gerwen had problems of his own with Peter 'Snakebite' Wright.

Born in Livingston, 13 miles west of Edinburgh, and based in Suffolk, Wright had played on the BDO circuit around a decade earlier, losing in the first round to Richie Burnett in the 1995 World Championship, and looked sensible enough while doing so.

But inspired by his favourite American wrestlers and with the help of wife Joanne, a hairdresser, Wright reinvented himself as one of the most colourful throwers on the PDC darts circuit.

Joanne styled his hair in a colourful mohican and dressed him in colourful clothes. "He dresses like a clown," said Wayne Mardle, "but he throws darts like a genius sometimes."

The outrageous hairdon'ts and clothes were a show of confidence – Wright was going to look really daft if he dressed up like that and couldn't play darts – and importantly, he also got the crowd on his side.

The walk-on music was 'Don't Stop the Party' and he encouraged the crowd to sing and dance along. Wright was here for a good time too.

Keen to get the crowd involved, he would every now and then pause in the middle of big checkouts and encourage them to raise the volume as he went for the double, the moment when most players needed silence.

Wright did things his way and it wasn't always to everyone else's liking.

Following a Premier League match that ended in a 7-7 draw, van Gerwen said Wright was "not professional".

Wright responded by telling van Gerwen to "grow up you big baby!"

In his defence, Wright, barely audible over his clothes, said he was just trying to entertain the crowd, nothing more than that, and if van Gerwen didn't like it, that was too bad.

Whether he clowned or not, Wright was good enough to give van Gerwen a game, but usually lost. The 2014 World Championship final was like that. Van Gerwen won a competitive match 7-4.

Similarly, when they met in the semi-finals of the European Championships earlier in November 2014, Wright had been a dart behind van Gerwen and lost a good match 11-7.

The World Series of Darts was a new prize on the PDC circuit in 2015.

It took the best players around the world – to Dubai, Japan, Perth, Sydney and Auckland – to compete against each other, and after the five tournaments the top eight players headed to Glasgow for the finals where they were joined by 12 invited players and a further four who came through a qualifying event in Coventry.

None of them looked to be playing well enough to stop van Gerwen at the Braehead Arena.

As he went through the tournament, he upped his average in every match, peaking with the 108.00 he recorded in his 11-5 semi-final win over Adrian Lewis that included an astonishing nine maximum 180s.

In the other semi-final, Wright, cheered on by a boisterous Scottish crowd, put out Taylor, reversing a loss in the final of the Japan event. But the record books showed that when he played van Gerwen, Wright rarely won.

Twelve of their previous 13 matches had gone van Gerwen's way and noticing the splodges of colour all over Wright's clothes, commentator Alan Warriner-Little said 'Snakebite' had "already lost in the world paintball championship".

He looked like losing the final of the World Series of Darts as well.

Wright rather gifted van Gerwen a break of throw in the first leg by missing three darts at a double, the second leg also went the Dutchman's way on double three and back-to-back 14-dart legs made it 4-0.

The crowd, silent throughout the opening four legs, found their voice in the fifth. Wright started with three successive 140s to set up a hold of throw.

The cheers were hushed by van Gerwen's first three darts of the sixth leg. They all landed in the treble 20, but he couldn't find the double he needed for 5-1, and from nowhere, Wright took out 121 on the bull's-eye to break the throw.

Those three darts changed the course of the match.

Wright was revived and, looking rather more like his flamboyant old self, he polished off an 86 checkout in the seventh leg with treble 18, double 16, the type of finish that had looked beyond him in the opening four legs.

That brought the score to 4-3 and Wright broke in the next to level the match.

Now it was van Gerwen who couldn't keep up with Wright.

The ninth leg also went to Wright – he was 5-4 up having been 4-0 down – and just when it seemed the match was running away from van Gerwen, he flung in a 170 – all in the middle – to tie the scores at 5-5 going into the interval when it looked as though Wright might go ahead 6-4.

What looked like another possible turning point wasn't.

Wright restarted the match with 180 and went on to hold his throw for 6-5. Van Gerwen then held after Wright missed three chances to break. 6-6.

If the legs kept going with the throw, Wright would win the match 11-10.

Van Gerwen had to break.

The break van Gerwen needed came in the 15th leg. It put him 8-7 ahead and gave him control of the match – but not for long.

Wright broke back immediately, taking out 116, with van Gerwen on 66, to tie the match at 8-8. It looked decisive. Van Gerwen was rattled and so poor was his aim at 20 and 19 in the 17th leg, he had to target 18 to find a treble. Under little pressure, Wright held for 9-8, but just when it seemed van Gerwen might be about to fall apart, he found the most brilliant of responses.

His first three darts of the 18th leg all landed in the treble 20 and he went on to hold for 9-9.

Still, the advantage was with Wright.

There were a maximum of three legs left – and should the match go its full distance, Wright would have the throw in the 19th and deciding 21st legs.

Van Gerwen got the chance of a break in the 19th leg – and missed.

"Big misses," reckoned commentator John Rawling after van Gerwen fired two darts wide of double 14.

Wright also struggled to hit the all-important double, finally finding double nine with his last dart for 10-9, leaving him one leg away from the match.

Van Gerwen had the throw in the 20th leg and left himself a 129 checkout that he really needed to take out with Wright sitting on a 90 checkout he was more than capable of finishing for the match.

The crowd's roars were hushed to an excited chatter as they settled themselves to watch what they had come to see. One of their own, Wright, was going to get a dart, possibly two, for the tournament.

Unless van Gerwen could take out 129 with his next three.

Even for a thrower of van Gerwen's ability, this was a finish he would only expect to polish off possibly once in every four or five attempts.

His first dart found 19 rather than the treble, leaving 110 and in a moment of 'blink and you'll miss it' magic, van Gerwen fired his next two darts into treble 20 and the bull's-eye and the match was saved.

These sorts of finishes from van Gerwen, reckoned Wayne Mardle, could leave his opponents with their "heads in a spin", but despite what van Gerwen had just thrown at him to deny him a match-winning opportunity, Wright held himself together well to start the 20th leg with back-to-back 140s and 100.

It wasn't enough.

Now at full throttle, van Gerwen answered with a blistering sequence of scores.

180, 134 and 137 left him 50 after only nine darts.

Wright had a shot at 121 for the match and fell well short, scoring just 28, and van Gerwen stepped up to nail 18 and double 16 to snatch it.

Van Gerwen, certain to lose a few minutes earlier, had won what Chris Mason called "one of the best finals I've seen in terms of quality and drama".

Warriner-Little, alongside Mason in the commentary box, said of van Gerwen: "He should buy a raffle ticket, he would probably win that as well," while Steve Palmer in the *Racing Post* took to calling van Gerwen "WGH", short for "World's Greatest Human".

Eric Bristow v Phil Taylor

1990 BDO World Championship final

IF Eric Bristow was going to be a darts coach, he was going to be the best darts coach.

"Ever since I was a kid I have wanted to be a winner," he said once. "At school, be it football, cricket or three miles cross-country, I had to drive myself to be the best."

In the 1980s, Bristow was the best darts player in the world.

He won five world championships, appeared in three more finals and in an era when darts was given more hours on television than football, he was one of sport's most recognisable faces.

Bristow was full of himself, dismissive of others. He would tell opponents "Hard luck mate" before matches, then stick his nose in the air and carry out the beating as promised.

Part Muhammad Ali – "the only bloke I have ever looked up to", wrote Bristow in his autobiography – part Artful Dodger, he wasn't to everyone's taste.

For Raymond van Barneveld and Kevin Painter, Bristow was a hero. "I liked his cockiness, his arrogance – and how good he was," said Painter.

Phil Taylor preferred more understated types. He rooted for Dave Whitcombe, John Lowe and Cliff Lazarenko and took a personal dislike to Bristow when he visited his 'Crafty Cockney' pub in Smallthorne, a couple of miles from his home in Stoke-on-Trent.

"I didn't like him at all," said Taylor. "He was too cocksure.

"Everyone sucked up to Eric and I didn't. I ignored him and he thought: 'What's up with him?' I was a cocky little bugger myself and that was the attraction."

Taylor had the attitude and, best of all, he was hungry.

"He'd come up from the gutter," wrote Bristow in his autobiography, "and was desperate to get out of his dead-end life."

Often, the Taylors – mother Betty, father Doug and Phil – would have to sleep on the floor of their two-bedroom council house because the stairs had been condemned by the council.

"We had a dartboard in our house," said Betty, "but that was about it. We would play darts and we were happy. I could not stand to lose and I passed this on to Phillip."

The young Taylor tried boxing – his grandfather was a bareknuckle fighter – but was better at dancing and showed a talent for darts.

"When I was a kid we didn't have a television – we didn't even have electricity – so everybody went to the community pubs for entertainment," he said, "and that's where I learnt to play darts. When I was 12, some old fella said to me that I'd be the greatest darts player in the world."

During a family holiday in Devon, Taylor beat Chris Johns, then ranked among the world's top 32, but it wasn't until a night out with girlfriend Yvonne and some friends that he took darts seriously.

He saw "a young lad from Biddulph" playing darts.

"I knew he had qualified for tournaments, but I remember watching him and saying: 'I can beat him.' Yvonne said: 'You don't play darts.' I said: 'I used to.' I ended up playing him and beating him and Yvonne bought me a set of darts for my birthday."

Whenever he got the chance, Taylor threw them and he threw them well enough to force his way into the Staffordshire side where his team-mates included Bristow.

Bristow was not the player he was.

Previously the most elegant of throwers, dartitis had robbed him of his fluency.

"One day I got up, tried a throw and realised I couldn't let go of the bloody thing," said Bristow. "I was gutted. I thought the only world I had known since I was 11 was gone."

Bristow was able to let go of his darts, but had to force them from his grip. The smooth, swan's neck pull back and release – "The Praying Mantis" was how Dave Lanning put it – was no more.

Although still a leading player, Bristow knew he would no longer dominate darts, leaving him "a bit lost" and in need of a new challenge.

Watching Taylor gave him an idea.

Bristow took a liking to Taylor and was impressed by his work ethic. "We played for hours and hours," said Bristow, "and I called him 'The Sponge'. He wanted to learn everything."

Bristow lent Taylor £9,000, enabling him to quit his job as a ceramic engineer in February 1988 and become a full-time darts professional.

Early on, there were more losses than wins – Bristow remembers John Lowe telling him he had wasted his money investing in Taylor – but Bristow was determined to make him a winner. Taylor thought he was ringing Bristow with good news after he had lost in a final, but

Bristow remembered his father telling him: "Nobody remembers the runners-up," and passed that on.

"Phil, don't phone me up to tell me you got beaten in the final," Taylor was told. "Next time you ring me up tell me you've won."

With that, Bristow hung up. He was similarly blunt after Taylor made his breakthrough by winning the Canadian Open in 1988, snatching his cheque from him when he left the stage, then reminding him how much more money was still owed.

Taylor paid off another chunk of the debt by qualifying for the 1990 World Championship and said he hoped to meet Bristow in the final. Although a 125/1 outsider to win the championship, Taylor had his backers in the Potteries.

"People were taking notice," he said. "I was young and a bit brash. Everyone was having bets on me."

A 3-1 pasting of No. 6 seed Russell Stewart in the first round kept Taylor's supporters interested, while Bristow shook off a determined challenge from Steve Gittins on the way to his ninth World Championship final.

There he would meet Taylor and before the match, BBC Television presenter Tony Gubba told viewers: "If Taylor wins it will be the biggest upset in the history of the Embassy..."

Paul Lim and Taylor had already ensured this World Championship would be remembered in the sport's record books.

Lim threw the tournament's first nine-darter in his second-round match against Jack McKenna and Taylor's average of 100.80 against Cliff Lazarenko in the semi-finals was the highest in the championship's history.

Despite Taylor's form, the bookmakers made Bristow the overwhelming favourite and Bristow himself predicted a 6-3 win. He would prove he was the world's best darts player, not just the world's best darts coach.

Though his methods were effective and had helped Taylor become only the second qualifier after Keith Deller to reach the World Championship final, Taylor secretly took exception to the way Bristow bullied and humiliated him and was desperate to claim the six sets he needed to pay off his debt and be freed from his grip.

"I wanted to be my own man," said Taylor, but in pre-match interviews 'The Crafty Potter' and 'The Crafty Cockney' gave identical answers. "Hit him hard and early" were the tactics.

Taylor's first two darts landed in the treble, the treble one that is, but he soon settled his nerves and corrected his aim and by the fifth leg he was throwing smoothly enough to take out a set-winning 170 finish that was an impressive statement of intent.

The second set started to a backdrop of excited chatter; it was only the fourth maximum finish in the championship's history.

Bristow won that second set, Taylor breezed to the third without reply and then the 180s started to fly in as they fought for control of the match.

There were eight maximums in just seven legs in the fourth and fifth sets – four apiece – but Taylor threw his at the crucial moments and, most importantly of all, took his chances.

His break of throw in the third leg of the fourth set was crucial. Previously, Bristow's mood had swayed between defiant and jovial, but now he looked troubled. Losing that leg meant that if Taylor held his throw, he would lead 4-1 and he did just that, wrapping up the fifth set with a 118 checkout in the deciding leg.

Twelve months earlier, Bristow had clawed his way back from 5-0 down to give Jocky Wilson a fright in the final and given his lack of big match experience, there was always a chance Taylor would wobble.

But players on the circuit had already noticed his toughness, his winning mentality and for all that Bristow had done for him, Taylor wouldn't show him any mercy.

Bristow had taught him too well for that.

A score of 4-1 to Taylor became 5-1 before there was finally hope for Bristow in the seventh set. Taylor missed three darts at doubles to win the match and Bristow smirked at the prospect of some mischief.

Bristow nicked that leg and was still smiling when he started the next, but Taylor wouldn't waste his chance and double ten gave him the World Championship and commentator Tony Green the opportunity to have his very own Kenneth "some people are on the pitch" Wolstenholme moment.

"Eric Bristow the champion in the Eighties, Phil Taylor the champion in the Nineties," he cried. "We have a new era in the sport of darts."

Bristow shook Taylor's hand, shared a joke with him, watched him pick up the trophy and a cheque for £24,000 – "I had never seen money like it in my life," said Taylor – then didn't speak to him for weeks.

Fifteen world titles later, Taylor admitted: "I never would have made it without him. I would have been working in a factory."

John Lowe v Bob Anderson

1988 BDO World Championship final

THROUGHOUT 1987, Bob Anderson and John Lowe duelled to be the best darts player on the planet.

They met in three finals that year, Anderson winning two of them.

That put 'The Limestone Cowboy' top of the world rankings, with Lowe not far behind.

Anderson did once have ambitions to throw bigger missiles – further.

He was selected to throw the javelin for Great Britain at the 1968 Olympics in Mexico, but said: "I broke bones in my elbow with a poor throw and a slip. So, I decided to throw small spears instead.

"I started playing darts at the age of five years old. My dad was a very good player and he taught me all about the game. We had a board on the back of the larder door."

Harry Anderson, known as 'Bob' for some reason, usually made it through a few rounds of the News of the World Individual championship and was well known around Winchester.

"Dad was known as 'Double top'," said Anderson. "That was his nickname. If Dad left double top, you put your darts away."

Anderson describes football as "my first love". A strapping centre-forward, he had trials for Brighton, Exeter and Southampton, along with cricket trials for Gloucestershire, but played most of his football in non-league with the likes of Woking and Farnborough Town.

His football career was ended by a knee injury and Anderson said: "When I couldn't play football any more, it left a huge void.

"I had to compete at something and I went back to playing darts.

"I started playing six nights a week. Whatever I did, I had to do it well. I had to give it 100 per cent. I hated losing. You show me someone who likes losing and I will show you a loser."

Anderson climbed up to No. 5 in the BDO rankings and a phone call from his accountant convinced him to quit his day job and pay the bills with his darts.

"My accountant rang me to say I had earned more in the last two months playing darts than I had made in two years working for the Civil Service," said Anderson. "It was a risk to resign, but if I hadn't taken it, I would have sat around thinking: 'I should have had a go.'"

Anderson became a full-time darts professional on 1 January 1985 and within a couple of years, 'The Limestone Cowboy' was No. 1 in the world.

Why 'The Limestone Cowboy'?

Unhappy the BDO were putting tape across sponsors' logos on players' shirts, Anderson decided he wanted to wear something different.

"I'm a massive John Wayne fan," he said, "and decided to wear a cowboy shirt.

"Boy, did I take some stick for that from Eric and Jocky.

"Sid Waddell called me 'The Limestone Cowboy' because I lived on the limestone hills in Wiltshire. Sid also called me 'Clint Plywood' and 'Wootton Bassett's answer to Burt Reynolds!'"

The cowboy he most resembled, reckoned Waddell, was Lee Van Cleef, the steely bad guy of many westerns, but Anderson also resembled his hero. Like Wayne, Anderson was a tough-as-old-boots gunslinger with a twinkle in his eye.

Always well turned out, Anderson, who gently leaned into an elegant throw with a whip-cracking action, was known on the circuit as a gentleman who played hard, but fair. He was always quick to offer congratulations when beaten. Which wasn't often in 1987.

For all the titles he won – the World Masters among them – the one Anderson really wanted was the World Championship.

He said he was "desperate" to win "the Embassy" at "the Lakeside" and seasoned oche observers said they had seldom seen a darter look as determined as Anderson was over those eight days in Frimley Green in 1988.

At the Lakeside, Anderson, beaten by Alan Evans in the quarter-finals 12 months earlier, was soon into his groove.

He lost the opening set of his first-round match to Bert Vlaardingerbroek, but didn't lose another on the way to the final and what's more, he posted the highest average in every round.

Following his semi-final whitewash of Rick Ney, the American said: "He blew me away like I wasn't even there."

Tony Gubba was clearly impressed, telling BBC viewers before the final that Anderson had produced "the most remarkably consistent series of results that anyone has ever put together on their way through to the final."

For Lowe, the defending champion, it was tougher. He had his struggles with Paul Reynolds and Eric Bristow, but both times he came through.

Against Bristow, Lowe came from 2-0 down to win, as he had in the previous year's final.

The 1988 final would be Lowe's seventh – he won in 1979 and 1987 – and Anderson's first.

Gubba told viewers the Lakeside was "a cauldron of excitement … noisy and hot."

This was a night when a cool head was needed. Anderson said: "We used to say you could drop a hand grenade on the ground behind John and he would still hit the double.

"He was so focused. He was hard to play against, but I enjoyed it. You knew he was going to be consistent and that kept you focused."

The crowd – or the vocal ones at least – were behind Lowe, described as "the housewives' choice" by Tony Green, but in the opening two sets, he won only one leg.

"I came out of the traps like a greyhound," was how Anderson remembered it.

Lowe consistently threw tons, but Anderson was hitting 140s, nine of them in the first two sets.

Lowe was quick to the oche in the third set, he was in a rhythm as well he fancied, and he won it without reply. 2-1.

The fourth set went to a deciding fifth leg.

Anderson got down to 121 after 12 darts and with Lowe sitting on 64, it looked like he needed to take it out.

Anderson missed the bull's-eye – "by an eighth of an inch" according to Waddell – but was reprieved after Lowe put his last dart just outside double 16.

Anderson blew his chance – missing two darts at double eight for 3-1 – and with his second dart, Lowe found the same target for 2-2.

Lowe had the darts in the fifth set – and Anderson soon took them off him.

He threw a maximum 180 in each leg on the way to winning the set without reply.

That put Anderson 3-2 up at the interval.

"Now all he's got to do is hold his throw," said Eric Bristow during the interval. "Sounds easy enough…"

The crowd were well behind Lowe. "Johnny Lowe, Johnny Lowe" they chanted to the tune of Eighties terrace anthem 'Here We Go' as the players returned for a sixth set that went to a deciding fifth leg.

Anderson, who missed a dart at double 16 in the previous leg for the set, had the throw for 4-2 and outscored Lowe to leave six darts to take out 161.

Six darts later, Anderson was on 40 and hoping Lowe wouldn't take out 118.

Lowe couldn't find the treble he needed to leave a double and though Anderson was short with his first dart at double 20, he put his next in double ten to stay in control of the match at 4-2.

Lowe really had to hold in the seventh and unlike the first, third and fifth sets, Anderson didn't put the Lowe throw under much pressure. Lowe won the set without reply to stay in touch at 4-3.

Given the way Lowe won the seventh set, he looked to have a chance of the break he needed in the eighth and a crowd who had been right behind him from the start cheered every treble he threw and groaned at every one he missed.

Anderson won the opening two legs, wired double top for 5-3 in the third and Lowe surged back to force a decider.

Anderson had the darts, but his tons weren't enough to keep Lowe at bay. After Anderson fell well short of a 141 checkout for 5-3, Lowe needed only one dart at double 16 for 4-4.

How the pro-Lowe crowd clapped and cheered.

Lowe had the darts in the ninth set and had to be feeling better about himself than Anderson was.

Anderson should have been 5-3 up and pressing for a match-winning break. Instead, it was 4-4, Lowe had the momentum, the darts and the crowd were on his side.

As he had to, Anderson cleared his thoughts and got on with the job of breaking Lowe's throw and seizing back control of what Waddell told viewers was "one of the great finals".

He did just that, throwing a pair of 140s in the opening leg to leave 36 with Lowe on 101.

Lowe missed, Anderson didn't – and Lowe was now chasing the game again.

Anderson held for 2-0, then Lowe held to set up a crucial fourth leg.

Lowe had to break or Anderson would lead 5-4 and have the darts for the match in the tenth set.

Anderson threw well enough to preserve his advantage in a neck-and-neck fourth leg to leave 62 – if Lowe didn't take out 161 with his next three darts. Lowe scored 95, leaving 66.

Anderson put his first dart in the dead centre of treble ten, leaving 32. His next landed just inside double 16 and without thinking too much, Anderson shifted his aim a centimetre or two and fired his last dart into the middle of double eight.

He was now 5-4 up and a hold of throw away from the World Championship.

But just when it seemed the match was Anderson's, Lowe had a chance to change the course of the game again in the first leg of that tenth set.

He missed a dart at double top, but with Anderson back on 110, it seemed likely Lowe would be back for another chance to break.

Anderson's first dart found treble 20 and the shot was on.

Left 50, he chose the 18, double 16 route and hit both for a dramatic hold of throw that must have hurt Lowe, who was just a dart away from a break.

"Finishing under pressure is tremendously important," said Anderson.

"You don't find many champions who can't do that. They are what win games. I wish I could have seen John's face when that went in!"

With that finish, Anderson resumed control of this most topsy-turvy of matches.

His eighth maximum helped him break Lowe's throw in the second leg and left him throwing for the match.

Anderson stayed ahead by finding the treble 20 a couple of times with his last dart and left 44 with Lowe on 60.

Anderson threw 12 to leave double 16 and with his last dart, he found it.

He was the champion of the world.

"Because of Phil Taylor, there aren't that many people who can say they have been a world champion at darts," reflected Anderson years later. "It's quite an achievement."

Adrian Lewis v
James Wade

KEITH Deller won the BDO World Championship in 1983 – and nothing much after that. Now he had a job in television and a wayward talent in need of his guidance.

Adrian Lewis had a sometimes misplaced sense of fun.

You knew Phil Taylor rolled his eyes when news reached him of Lewis's late-night karaoke knees-up during the World Matchplay in Blackpool. Taylor, formerly his mentor, had taught him better than that. Taylor said darts' *enfant terrible* had to grow up – and Deller decided to help him do it.

Deller sensed the chance to exorcise his own demons through Lewis. "I was at the top of darts, but I blew it," he said. "I was in the papers every day, I appeared on *Bullseye*, *Surprise Surprise* and even *This Is Your Life*. I didn't even have to queue to get into Stringfellows."

For the benefit of younger readers, that was all a big deal back then. Deller continued: "I've got so much experience on what to do and what not to do as a darts player.

"I lived the party lifestyle and just did too much media stuff which took my eye off the game and I was punished for it.

"Adrian is the same. I believe he can be the next darts millionaire and I want to make sure he does. It'll make up for me missing out on it."

For a few weeks, Deller just watched Lewis – and wasn't impressed by much of what he saw.

"Adrian was always very dedicated in practice," he said, "but wasn't getting it right on match days.

"I remember a Players Championship over in Las Vegas when Adie was due to play Co Stompe.

"The game was due on and he was chatting to a couple of blokes who were over from England. He went 4-0 down to Co and ended up losing. Afterwards he came over to me and said: 'I don't understand it.' I said: 'Well I can. You need to be ready to play. You need to be ready to kick in with 180, 140, 140.'

"Tournaments are business. I used to walk past practice rooms and hear him laughing and joking. I don't any more."

Deller made sure he sent Lewis into every match in the right frame of mind. He said: "We get on the practice board an hour before Adrian goes on stage.

"Adrian is so laid back he could fall over and I have to get him focused. When he goes on stage I want him believing there's nobody better than him."

Then there was the walk on...

Deller had watched Lewis "running to the stage. He was wearing himself out. I told him the way he was running around he should have had a basketball in his hand!

"The top players are all focused. They have their heads ready and don't concentrate on waving to the crowd. You don't want to be the bloke who is jollying around."

To get the best out of Lewis, Deller also kept him busy. Lewis would joke about his increased exhibition workload after Deller took on the job of managing him, but it kept the money coming in, kept him throwing, kept him sharp.

Whatever else Deller did, it worked and in January 2011 Lewis won the PDC World Championship at Alexandra Palace after starting the tournament as a 33/1 outsider.

His thrilling 7-5 win over Gary Anderson secured the winner's cheque for £200,000 and included the first perfect nine-dart leg in a World Championship final.

The 20 maximum 180s Lewis threw during the match took his total for the tournament to a record 60 and by winning the sport's biggest prize at the age of 25, he became the youngest winner of the PDC world title in its 17-year history.

But it didn't look like he was going to keep the World Championship.

In the first round of the 2012 tournament, Lewis came from 2-0 down to beat Leamington undertaker Nigel Heydon in a fifth-set tiebreak and struggled to a 4-2 win over Robert Thornton in the last 32.

Thornton was millimetres away from taking the match into a seventh and deciding set and Eric Bristow snapped afterwards: "He's not playing like a world champion.

"He will make a mistake against someone and get caught out. He's throwing bad darts, then saying 'Rubbish' to himself when he should just forget about it and get on with it.

"He's throwing a bit too fast and throwing too many loose darts. He's missing trebles by a long way.

"I think Lewis will come through against Jones in the next round, but then his problems start when he comes up against the big hitters who average 100. Too many players will punish him for playing like that."

Lewis did come through against Wayne Jones 4-0 and after a first-round struggle, James Wade also started to show his best form.

Wade was a tortured talent. Even when he was winning – and he had won six major televised tournaments – he said he didn't enjoy darts.

And after he lost to Austrian Mensur Suljovic in the second round of the 2011 World Championship, Wade spent four weeks in The Priory clinic battling depression, including a spell on suicide watch.

Wade finally found some comfort in darts and declared his demons defeated after back-to-back whitewashes of Jelle Klaasen and Steve Farmer set up a quarter-final against John Part at Alexandra Palace.

Part, the three-time world champion, took him all the way to a fifth and deciding set tiebreak that Wade held himself together to win.

Lewis also survived a nerve-jangling quarter-final. He beat Terry Jenkins 5-3 after the antiques dealer from Herefordshire had wiped out his 3-0 lead – and his semi-final against Wade promised more drama, both darting and human.

Lewis and Wade had exchanged unpleasantries during the final of the World Grand Prix in 2010 and after his loss, Lewis predicted: "I'm sure we're going to meet in lots of finals – and James won't win many more."

Lewis usually reacted badly to Wade and the crowd, however, and in the semi-finals of the World Championship, they were both against him.

Going into their match at Alexandra Palace, Wade had a 100 per cent record against Lewis in knockout tournaments and Lewis's criticism of the crowd following his quarter-final victory over Jenkins meant they wanted to see him beaten.

There were cheers when Wade won the opening set against the throw, but Lewis responded and had a dart at double top to break back immediately and level the match. He missed and complained to officials about a breeze blowing across the stage that was pushing his darts off target.

Wade also seemed distracted. He paused before he threw, but still threw well enough to nail the set-winning double.

TAKING AIM ... Keith Deller, the 1983 BDO world champion

ON TOP OF THE WORLD ... AGAIN ... Eric Bristow celebrates victory over John Lowe in the 1985 BDO World Championship final

HOW DOES HE DO IT? The unorthodox Jocky Wilson on his way to the 1989 BDO World Championship

WHO SAYS PHIL TALE IS UNBEATABLE? John Part celebrates during the World Final

JUST CHAMPION! Jelle Klaasen has just beaten Raymond van Barneveld in the 2006 BDO World Championship final

YEEEESSSS! Raymond van Barneveld has just hit the target in the 2007 PDC World Championship final against Phil Taylor

WHAT A MATCH! Martin 'Wolfie' Adams throws and Phill Nixon watches during the 2007 BDO World Championship final

GET IN THERE! Phil Taylor celebrates hitting the match-winning double in the 2009 PDC World Championship final against Raymond van Barneveld

COUNT ME IN ... Ted 'The Count' Hankey in action against Tony O'Shea in the 2009 BDO World Championship final

POINTING THE WAY TO VICTORY ... James Richardson is on his way to a huge upset win over Raymond van Barneveld in the 2012 PDC World Championship

CAN YOU FEEL A DRAUGHT? *James Wade and Adrian Lewis during the 2012 PDC World Championship semi-final*

THE VIKING'S AIM IS TRUE ... *Andy Fordham on the way to the 2014 BDO World Championship*

GAME! SHOT! And another leg to Lisa Ashton during the 2014 BDO Women's World Championship

NIP AND TUCK ... Phil Taylor celebrates and Gary Anderson sees the funny side during their epic 2015 PDC World Championship final

UPSETTING THE ODDS ... Raymond van Barneveld has just toppled 'Mighty' Michael van Gerwen during the 2016 PDC World Championship

HEAVENS ABOVE! Michael van Gerwen has just won the 2017 PDC World Championship

The cause of the problem appeared to be identified and a pair of doors at the side of the stage were shut. But the breeze persisted and both players left the stage during the first leg of the third set.

"James mentioned it before I did," said Lewis. "I have light darts and the breeze was blowing them around. I missed tops for the second set and was fuming when I went off stage."

Lewis had lost his composure and later admitted he would have lost the match 6-0 had they stayed on the stage.

As the delay stretched towards 20 minutes there was talk of Lewis forfeiting the match, but he returned, just as he did after his walk-off during his World Championship quarter-final against Peter Manley in 2006, and what's more, he won the third set.

Wade hit back to win the next three and at 5-1 ahead, he was just one set away from the final.

Although Lewis pegged it back to 5-2, Wade had the throw in the eighth set and after the opening exchanges in the deciding fifth leg he had six darts to finish 168 for the match.

That became 108 and after starting his checkout attempt with treble five, Wade's next dart found treble 19 to leave him one dart at double 18 for a place in the final.

His dart landed just inside the wire – and everything changed.

The near-miss jolted Lewis out of his mediocrity and focused his thoughts. "I told myself: 'I'm not giving up my title that easily,'" he said.

Lewis stepped up to take out 98 in two darts to win the set and trim the gap to 5-3. He whirled around to share his relief with the crowd before leaving the stage for a break.

Wade had been just millimetres away from a place in the final of the World Championship and that thought must have crossed his mind many times in the minutes he spent backstage before the start of the ninth set.

Lewis, so close to defeat just a few moments earlier, was thinking more positively. He said: "When I got it back to 5-3, I told myself to really go at him. I was a different player when I came back on stage."

Wade was a different player as well. The momentum had shifted.

Lewis, throwing quicker, looking more purposeful, breezed through the ninth set in just five minutes without allowing Wade a dart at a double.

"He wasn't hitting the same scores he was in the first six sets," said Lewis. "He wasn't having shots at doubles."

Lewis got used to winning legs and Wade got used to losing them.

Wade had the throw in the tenth set – and missed two darts at a double to win the opening leg after Lewis started with back-to-back maximums.

Lewis won the set without reply to send the match into a decisive 11th set and by then, he didn't think he could miss.

Even when he did miss, Wade couldn't shake himself out of his slump to take advantage. Lewis's finishing deserted him in the second leg and handed Wade seven chances to hold his throw. He missed the lot.

Lewis finally found double one with his eighth dart at a double and went on to add an exclamation mark to the greatest comeback in darts history with a 161 checkout that clinched a 6-5 win and a place in the final.

The match-winning bull's-eye was nailed at 12.45am and for a few moments after that, Lewis stood on the stage with his hands on his hips, trying to take in what he had just achieved…

He had turned a 5-1 deficit into a 6-5 triumph; winning ten successive legs after Wade missed a dart at double 18 to beat him 6-2.

After a few hours' sleep, Lewis was back on the practice board and he went on to beat Andy Hamilton 7-3 in the final to become only the third player after Eric Bristow and Raymond van Barneveld to retain the World Championship 12 months after first winning it.

PIT Chris Mason and Ted Hankey against each other and anything could happen...

In the 1999 BDO World Championship, Mason had won a second-round match at the Lakeside Country Club 3-1 by playing less poorly than Hankey in a disappointing spectacle remembered for a plethora of missed doubles.

Twelve months later, they met again in the semi-finals – and it was a very different match...

Mason and Hankey were both combustible, unpredictable talents.

Often described as a confidence player, Mason was close to unbeatable at his best and close to tears when he wasn't, while Hankey was all sovereign rings, stroppiness and snarls – whether he hit or missed. All an act to motivate himself, reckoned Tony O'Shea, who knew Hankey better than most.

He remembers playing a prank on Hankey when they shared a caravan. O'Shea threw his shoes on the roof of their caravan for a laugh – shortly before the heavens opened and they were drenched in a downpour.

"Ted doesn't wear socks," said O'Shea, "so he ended up playing barefoot!"

Hankey saw the funny side.

As well as being good fun, Hankey was also an articulate, thoughtful interviewee, much nicer than you might imagine.

Nonetheless, Hankey, likened to "a Dickensian gravedigger" by commentator John Rawling, was also more than happy to embrace his dark side.

Given the nickname 'The Count' after getting the part of Dracula in the school play when he was 12 years old, he threw plastic bats into the crowd on his way to the stage and sometimes, they threw insults back at him.

Hankey had his supporters as well, none louder than his mum.

Every televised match Hankey played, cameras zoomed in on Janet screaming encouragement, burying her head in her hands or celebrating.

"I shout because I have to," she explained. "I know he can do it and just want him to do it."

Wins over Bob Taylor, Steve Douglas and Kevin Painter – dropping just two sets along the way – gave Janet plenty to shout about, but still Mason went into the best-of-nine-sets semi-final as the favourite for the championship.

In the first round, he had ended Raymond van Barneveld's hopes of a third successive World Championship with a 100.02 average that was the best of the tournament.

That was followed by wins over Matt Clark and Andy Fordham.

"Fordham was a form horse," remembered Mason, "a real grinder. After I beat him, I thought it was my time."

John Part, commentating for the BBC, sensed 'needle' between the players at the start of the semi-final and whatever was in the air that night, it went up a notch when Hankey's second throw brought him 180.

By the end of the second set, he had thrown four more maximums, had an average of 102.88 – and found himself 2-0 down.

Mason had been more consistent and took every chance, every half-chance that came his way, celebrating every winning double with a 'what did you expect?' shrug.

But then Mason's darts started veering off target and Hankey hardly missed for the next five legs – until he threw to win the fourth set.

Hankey missed eight darts at a double for 2-2 and Mason snatched it for a 3-1 lead.

The interval came at the right time for Hankey, who returned with his thoughts clear to throw two more maximums on his way to winning the fifth set.

Mason hit back to hold his throw for 4-2, just one set away from winning the match.

The scoreline seemed to set Hankey free.

"I had lost the game and had nothing to lose," he said, "so I just threw my darts – and they went in.

"There was no pressure on me. I just played the game. I didn't think about what I was doing because I was going to lose the game."

Hankey raced to the seventh set 3-0, wrapping it up with a 12-dart leg that included his 17th maximum 180, a record for a match in the 23-year history of the BDO World Championship.

How does he do it?

Hankey explained: "Get the first one in, then just throw. Don't change anything, don't think, just throw and they will go in.

"The worst thing you can do is think about it. Just throw them naturally and if you're good enough they will go in."

For all Hankey's 180s, Mason just had to hold his throw in the eighth set – as he had done in the second, fourth and sixth sets – and the match was his.

Hankey missed two darts for a break in the first leg – and it looked like he wouldn't get another chance in the third leg.

Mason left himself 16 after just nine darts with Hankey way back on 193.

But when it mattered most, Mason started missing.

He missed three darts at a double, then missed three more after Hankey piled on the pressure with another maximum.

Hankey mopped up 13 for the crucial break and went on to level the match at 4-4 after Mason missed two darts at double top.

Somehow, a match that Mason had largely controlled was going to a final set and, what's more, Hankey had the throw and the momentum going into the decider having wiped out a 4-2 deficit.

Hankey held his throw in the opening leg of the ninth set with the help of his 20th maximum 180 and another 180 in the next gave him a chance of the break he needed if he was to win the deciding set without going to a tiebreak.

Mason still had first throw at a double, but missed, then Hankey missed twice.

But he found double six with his last dart and that put him 2-0 ahead in the set and a leg away from the final.

Mason missed two at double top to save the match and at the fifth attempt, Hankey won it with double five.

Hankey mopped the sweat from his brow while the Hankeys in the crowd – mum Janet and wife Lorna – shook their fists and screamed with joy.

Hankey finished the match with a World Championship record of 22 maximum 180s and Mason threw 11.

The statisticians revealed that Hankey threw more 180s (22) than doubles (20).

"That is unbelievable darts," Bobby George told television viewers.

In the final, Hankey met Ronnie Baxter, the fast-throwing No. 2 seed who had beaten Scott Wollaston, Bobby George, Colin Monk and Co Stompe.

Hankey promised "more fireworks than you saw on 31 December, 1999", then started the match with a throw of 45 and took 26 darts to win the opening leg.

Nine more maximum 180s later – taking his total to a championship record 48 – he finished the match with a 170 checkout, then collapsed to the floor.

He said: "I hit the 170 and thought: 'No way! I haven't!' I was expecting to wake up."

Eric Bristow v Bobby George

1980 BDO World Championship final

"THE match that changed darts," was how Eric Bristow put it.

"Everyone knew we had skill," he said, "and now they knew we were characters as well ..."

As you will probably know, Leighton Rees won the inaugural World Championship in 1978 and the following year, John Lowe lifted the trophy. Neither impressed Bobby George much.

"Leighton was a lovely fella," said George, "but nobody outside Wales could understand what he was saying.

"And John used to carry a briefcase and wear a bowler hat!"

The drinking classes who played and followed darts, George reckoned, would be more excited and rather better represented by flashy, streetwise wide boys – and as luck would have it, he happened to know of a couple...

"I had the candles and the glitter," said Bobby, "and Eric had the mouth."

"Two poseurs," was how Bristow put it. "We were the first to give darts razzmatazz."

Bristow, his shoulders sloping and a cigarette glued to his bottom lip, had a repertoire of put-downs that were as sharp as his darts.

"He had 'BG' on his shirt," said Bristow of George, "and I said it stood for 'Big Girl'. I said he should change it to 'BGB' for 'Big Girl's Blouse.'"

Not that anything Bristow said could ever bother George.

"Eric couldn't get under my skin," he said. "I had known him since he was a kid.

"He would try to wind me up. If we went to a three-day tournament, Eric would ask me if I had bought a day return ticket on the train, things like that. But it was just a bit of banter, part of the game."

Bristow always had something to say and a glint in his eye. He called the dart "my sixth finger" and he never expected to miss. He rarely practised throwing at the lower doubles such as four and two because he reasoned that "good players don't end up on those doubles".

Often, Bristow needed only one dart at double 16.

George, part 'Del Boy' Trotter from BBC sitcom *Only Fools and Horses*, part Liberace, cracked jokes in his 'chewing gravel' accent and was photographed with cigars, champagne and shirtless. Never knowingly understated, he had a sense of style that was uniquely his own.

George and Bristow first met when both played in the Walthamstow League and went on to be pairs partners. George would spend his days laying granite floors – "tough work, but good money", he remembered – then pack his tools into the back of his Cortina and pick up Bristow.

"We went to tournaments, hustled to make a few quid," said Bobby. "That was our apprenticeship."

The apprenticeship included a scrape at the Mother Hubbard pub in Loughton after a penniless Bristow was left owing local thrower Bob Wood £200.

"I offered to play him double or nothing," said George, "but I didn't have any money either.

"I told Eric to move the car round to the front of the pub so we could clear off straight after the game. He said he couldn't drive and the locals didn't look too friendly…"

Fortunately, George won the match and the pair made their escape.

Bristow started playing darts with his father, George, when he was 11 years old and by the time he was 14 he was regularly winning money matches against the locals at the Arundel Arms in Stoke Newington.

Bristow was 17 years old when he won his first tournament – the Sussex Open – and victories in the British Open in 1978 and the World Masters in both 1977 and 1979 enabled him to leave his job in a clothing factory to play darts full-time.

He went into the inaugural World Championship in 1978 as the No. 1 seed – and went out in the opening match to Conrad Daniels from the USA.

George, who didn't start playing until he was 30, didn't even get as far as the first round of the World Championship in 1978. He wasn't invited to take part in the qualifiers – and missed out again the following year before winning both the North American Open and News of the World International to secure his place in the tournament in 1980.

His prize for winning the North American Open in 1978 was $4,000 and an all-expenses paid trip to London. The sponsors saved a few quid because at the time, George lived in Ilford, a short train ride from the capital.

By the time the World Championship started in February 1980, George was earning enough money to be a full-time professional and had his image all worked out.

He owed his image to a boozy night in Spain spent watching an Elvis impersonator.

"He was useless," chuckled Bobby, "but these women liked him because he looked good. I thought: 'I can play darts badly and people will still remember me.'"

That gave George an idea.

Gordon Croucher was the landlord of the King George V pub in Gants Hill and his daughter was a dressmaker.

Bobby asked her to restyle his darts shirt and she put together a sequined shirt.

"The gaffer bet me £25 I wouldn't wear it on stage," said George. "But it got the women watching. I was fitter and slimmer in those days."

George was clearly determined to turn heads. He walked to the stage to the tribal, call-to-arms thump of 'I'm the Leader of the Gang (I Am)'.

"I did the first walk-on," he said. "They said I made it a circus, that it was all wrong. I was just trying to make it more enjoyable to watch.

"We had the music, the walk-on and when I hit a maximum, I would jump in the air and shout: 'Yeeeeaaahhhh!'

"I never thought darts would become as big as it has. I think we helped make it that way."

George showed there was substance behind his showmanship by reaching the World Championship final at the first attempt with wins over Dave Whitcombe, Leighton Rees and Cliff Lazarenko.

Lazarenko had ended Lowe's world title defence in the second round and Bristow, never beyond the quarter-finals in the two previous World Championships, was also feeling the pressure.

"It was the one thing I wanted," he said. "I'd won all the other major titles, but never the worlds. I just wanted to get it out the way and win the damn thing."

Not the words you would expect from the most confident of throwers and there were no signs of anxiety or self-doubt in his whitewashes of Tony Clark and Jocky Wilson.

The 22-year-old's semi-final was tougher – a 4-3 win over Tony Brown – and set up a best-of-nine-sets final against George.

"Eric was good," said Bobby, "but I had beaten him up loads of times. I thought I would beat him."

Although they knew each other well, Bristow did manage to unsettle George before the match.

"Eric was saying I had written a poem I was planning to read out if I won," said Bobby. "I didn't know what he was talking about. I hadn't written a poem."

The crowd were sucked into the back-and-forth drama and swapped chants while their favourites traded trebles on the stage.

"If I made a mistake, he took it out," said George and after 20 successive legs went with the throw, the scores were tied at 3-3.

The crucial break came in the opening leg of the seventh set. Bristow took out 101 with George waiting on 25 and 12 darts later, 'The Crafty Cockney' was on the brink of a 4-3 lead.

George held his throw in the third leg and had a dart at the bull's-eye to take the set into a deciding fifth leg.

He missed and Bristow took out 44 for a 4-3 lead. Bristow had the crucial break and celebrated by having a few gulps of his pint, then started conducting the crowd's chants.

Bristow knew if he held his throw in the eighth set he would be the world champion.

The opening two legs went with the darts, then George took out 121 to break Bristow's throw and his clenched teeth celebration showed how much it meant.

He was back in the match.

In the next leg, Bobby would throw to make it 4-4.

Both players stumbled in that fourth leg.

Bristow couldn't hide his disgust when he threw 41, but George couldn't take advantage.

He missed 110 for the set and Bristow took out his favourite double 16 to throw for the match.

But back-to-back scores of 45 and 82 handed George three darts at 141 for the set.

Bobby left himself 18 and got a chance to save the match after Bristow missed a dart at double top for the championship.

George dragged his first dart into single nine, took aim at one to leave double four and hit 20 instead.

"I was thinking about the next set," admitted Bristow, "then all of a sudden, I had a chance I wasn't expecting.

"I told myself: 'You might only get one shot at it in your whole life.'"

Bristow dragged his first dart under double 20 – "I told myself: 'Don't let it go to the last dart'" – and his next was "the best double ten I ever threw".

The World Championship – and the £4,500 first prize – was his.

Asked for his opinion on George, Bristow, a glint in his eye and cigarette smoke swirling around him, smirked: "He's the No. 2 of the future."

Bristow was No. 1 – and planning to stay there.

Michael van Gerwen v Raymond van Barneveld

2016 PDC World Championship third round

NO wonder Michael van Gerwen was the favourite to win the 2016 PDC World Championship.

In 2015, he captured 18 titles – including six majors – and at Alexandra Palace in December, he set out to win the biggest for a second time.

Van Gerwen was given a first-round fright by René Eidams, a bespectacled German qualifier unrecognisable outside his own neighbourhood who took the world No. 1 to a fifth-set tiebreak from 2-0 down.

Van Gerwen came through it and went on to post a 109.23 average in a second-round savaging of Darren Webster, bettered only by Phil Taylor, with 111.21 and 110.94, in the history of the PDC World Championship.

Not since Taylor was in his unplayable pomp had there been a darter as ruthless as van Gerwen. Winning wasn't enough for him. He had to destroy his opponents. Van Gerwen couldn't hide his disgust when Webster nicked a leg off him.

That was van Gerwen's 25th consecutive win on television – another record only bettered by Taylor with 29 – and following the whitewash of Webster, who didn't play badly, the bookmakers made van Gerwen an odds-on favourite to lift the Sid Waddell Trophy for the second time in three years. The odds on van Barneveld were longer.

The van Barneveld who beat Phil Taylor in the match of all matches in 2007 hadn't been seen too often since, but when his mind was right and his stars were aligned, at 48 years old, he was still some player.

Not that he had shown it recently.

Without a major title since he captured the 2014 Premier League, van Barneveld was seeded 16th at Alexandra Palace – and was in danger of losing his place in the top 16.

He had other things on his mind as well. On the afternoon of his second-round match with Stephen Bunting, van Barneveld learned he had become a grandfather, daughter Patty giving birth to a boy, Mason.

But rather than distract van Barneveld, it seemed to drive him on to outlast Bunting over seven back-and-forth sets – despite 15 maximum 180s from Bunting.

That set up the match with van Gerwen and, though van Barneveld was fancied to lose, if there was a match that would bring out the best in him, it was surely this one.

He was playing the world No. 1 – and a fellow Dutchman – at the World Championship for a place in the quarter-finals.

In a mischievous moment the night before, Phil Taylor claimed van Barneveld had a 'hoodoo' over van Gerwen, but the record books showed that of the 14 matches van Gerwen and van Barneveld played in 2015, van Gerwen won 11.

There were those who bet on a van Gerwen whitewash. To them, this looked like a match between a once great champion on the way down and another apparently close to his peak.

Van Barneveld knew what was being said and that's why he kept away from social media before the World Championship. "It does hurt," he said of what was written about him. "I put darts on the map in Holland and maybe I deserve more credit for that."

Van Barneveld had done a lot for darts in Holland, but not, it appeared, for van Gerwen.

"I don't look up to anyone," he told Sky Sports before the match.

"If you look up to someone, you're already 2-0 down."

The same interviewers found the oft-troubled van Barneveld in a truculent mood. He reckoned the set format didn't really suit van Gerwen and added that he had no fear of anyone in the championship. Privately, van Barneveld fed himself only positive thoughts: that he had beaten van Gerwen three times in the last year, that Eidams had given him a scare in the first round. He was thinking like a winner.

Van Barneveld was up for the fight.

Not only was he thinking and talking well, van Barneveld also looked better having shed four stones over the previous four years.

"The funny thing is," said van Barneveld, "when I was 135kg [21 stones] I played a lot better – and I won an awful lot more."

To beat van Gerwen, he surely needed a good start.

Van Barneveld had the darts in the first set and threw them well enough. He averaged 105.40, but most visits, van Gerwen found two trebles, sometimes three, and he wasn't missing doubles either.

He broke in the first leg of the match with a 127 checkout and went on to win the set.

Van Barneveld rose to the challenge and the second set was very different. He kept leaving a finish after nine darts and van Gerwen couldn't stay with him. Van Barneveld wobbled a bit on the doubles, but found them eventually to level the match with a break.

"Yeeeeeahhhh!" bellowed van Barneveld and the 'Barney Army' went bananas, belting out their anthem at full volume as the players left the stage for a break.

Darts crowds loved to watch van Gerwen, so fast and fearless, but they loved van Barneveld.

The third set went to a deciding leg and van Barneveld held after his first nine darts – seven of which found big trebles – left him on 64.

The fourth set also went with the throw. Van Barneveld's scoring dipped – he averaged around 90 – and that allowed van Gerwen to hold without reply, breaking in the second leg with a whirlwind 170 checkout.

The next break went van Gerwen's way in the third leg of the fifth set – and it left him throwing for a 3-2 lead.

He left 32 with van Barneveld way back on 124 – and needing to take it out.

Like a great champion, van Barneveld found treble 20, treble 14 and double 11 for what commentator Rod Studd reckoned was "one of the greatest checkouts ever seen at Alexandra Palace".

Van Barneveld followed it with a hold of throw that clinched the set for 3-2.

Just as good as van Barneveld's 124 was van Gerwen's 135 that snatched a sensational sixth set and saved the match.

When van Gerwen took aim, van Barneveld was sitting on 121 for the match – and the way he was throwing, it looked to be within his range.

Van Gerwen didn't give him a chance, nailing bull's-eye, treble 15 and double top to send the match into a deciding seventh set.

Van Barneveld held in the opening leg with a 101 checkout – and van Gerwen cracked.

Of his next six darts, only one found a big treble.

Van Gerwen recovered to get down to 53, but van Barneveld had a shot at 72 for a break and with many of the crowd on their feet, he put his last dart in double nine.

Surely there was no way back for van Gerwen now, but he put together a ten-darter to break back and a match he seemed certain to lose was back in the balance.

Michael van Gerwen v Raymond van Barneveld

Van Gerwen had the darts – and the momentum – in the fourth leg.

He scored well enough, but couldn't shake off van Barneveld and when he missed a dart at double top, it handed van Barneveld a chance at 96 for the match.

He needed only two darts – the first hit treble 20, the second double 18 – and he jumped for joy.

"That was darts at its very, very best," was how Wayne Mardle put it and alongside him in the Sky Sports commentary box, Rod Studd described the previous hour's drama as "arguably the greatest match ever played on the Alexandra Palace stage".

Ted Hankey v
Tony O'Shea

2009 BDO World Championship final

THE Eighties belonged to Eric Bristow, Phil Taylor dominated the Nineties and maybe the Noughties would be Ted Hankey's?

Days into the new millennium, he raced to the BDO World Championship with a 46-minute whitewash of Ronnie Baxter, adding an exclamation mark to the shortest final in history with a 170 checkout.

Overwhelmed, Hankey flopped to his knees...

"I didn't deliberately leave 170," he said years later. "In exhibitions I had been leaving 170 and could never hit it... darts is a strange game."

As for the Hankey era, it didn't happen.

Twelve months later, he reached the final again, losing to John 'Boy' Walton, but with fewer televised tournaments on the BDO circuit and more mouths to feed, he had to go out "labouring, working in supermarkets, anything to pay the bills, to keep the family going..."

In the nine years since he won the World Championship, Hankey also got divorced, remarried and gave up drinking...

For all that had changed, something hadn't. Hankey still couldn't beat Tony O'Shea in a major tournament.

O'Shea and Hankey went way back...

O'Shea started playing darts when the landlord at his local, the Church Inn in Stockport, doubled the price of a frame of pool to 20 pence.

Encouraged by handing Alan Evans "a couple of good hidings" in the Stockport & District League, the affable greenkeeper decided to take darts more seriously – most of the time.

To keep himself and his team-mates amused on the way to county matches, O'Shea would 'moon' at passing cars and was even known to share a joke or two with Hankey.

"I met Ted at the holiday camps and open events in the early days," said O'Shea, "and we all knew how good he was. We said he would be a world champion..."

In 2000, Hankey did become world champion, but in the following five years, O'Shea beat him twice at the Lakeside Country

Club; in the first round in 2003, then in the quarter-finals two years later.

Going into the 2009 championship, O'Shea looked to be throwing possibly the best darts of his career.

Months earlier, he had won the Welsh Open and in the quarter-finals at Frimley Green, he put out No. 1 seed Gary Anderson, who chucked his darts into the lake in frustration.

Think of 'oche rage' and you probably think of Hankey.

Passive aggressive on the oche and much nicer than you might imagine off it, he was once warned for punching the board and was known to squabble with the crowd.

For a week in January 2009, this volatile talent held himself together to beat Brian Woods, Ross Montgomery, John Walton and Martin Adams to reach the BDO World Championship final.

The crowd were on O'Shea's side, just the way Hankey likes it…

"It's part of Ted's game plan," said O'Shea of Hankey's volatile relationship with the darts public. "It's for him, not the crowd. It's how he gets his head on. It's how Ted motivates himself. He is a bit misunderstood."

Hankey had never beaten O'Shea on stage in a major tournament, but it didn't bother him. "Tony had been having the better of me for 20 years," he said, "but I believe in percentages. I thought: 'He can't keep beating me.'"

Clearly there wasn't that much between them and in their biggest match yet, over the best of 13 sets, Hankey opened up a 4-2 lead.

The next four sets went with the throw and at 6-4 ahead, Hankey was just a set away from the World Championship.

O'Shea, wearing the blue and white of Stockport County, had the darts in the 11th set, but Hankey broke in the opening leg, then held his throw and in the third leg, he was 62 points away from the match.

He made a mess of what could have been a two-dart finish – and didn't even get a dart at a double after missing single 12.

O'Shea snatched the leg and Hankey went to pieces in the decider, leaving his lead a slender one at 6-5.

The crowd chanted: "Tony! Tony!"

"I had never heard noise like it at a darts match," remembered O'Shea. "I had written the game off twice, but Ted missed a few doubles and I hung in there."

But if there was to be a deciding 13th set, O'Shea would have to break the throw, and at 2-0 down he had to win the next three legs or the match would be lost.

Hankey got to the finish first in the third leg, had a dart at double top for a 120 checkout and the match – and missed.

O'Shea had to take out 84 to stay in the match – and did. With his last dart.

That double six must have hurt Hankey – but he soon got over it. In the deciding leg of the 12th set, he threw for the match, started with a maximum 180 and turned to glare at the crowd. Hankey was back. That maximum helped him pull away and with O'Shea back on 224, he had six darts to take out 81 for the match.

Hankey missed two darts at double top, one at double ten, then came back and was off target at double five and double two.

Six missed chances to win the World Championship...

O'Shea took out 84 by finding double six with his last dart for 6-6 and that sent him bouncing around the stage, while Hankey ruefully scratched his ear and raised his eyebrows.

Hankey, it seemed, had blown it.

Again, the crowd, sniffing a sensation, chanted "Tony! Tony!" and their hero bit his lip, and couldn't wait for the final set to start. A couple of feet away, Hankey was keeping his head when all about him were losing theirs.

For all the talk in the commentary box about the momentum being with O'Shea, Hankey's mindset was the better one.

"The crowd cheering for Tony worked in my favour," he reasoned. "If they shout for him, the pressure is on him. I became the underdog."

O'Shea, sweaty, anxious, so close to what he'd always wanted, had the darts, but twitched when he threw them and Hankey grabbed the opening leg.

He was back in front – but not for long.

O'Shea broke back instantly, meaning that after more than two hours, the scores were still level and the match was in the balance.

The next shift went Hankey's way.

His 15th maximum 180 of the match helped him break – and if Hankey held his throw in the next leg, the match was his.

"The sweat was dripping off me," remembers O'Shea, "and instead of drying my hands, my head and my darts I just carried on.

"I was a bit excited and just wanted to get on with it."

Hankey's opening throw of 60 in the fourth leg handed O'Shea an opening, but he could reply with just 15 and this time, Hankey didn't let him escape. He left himself six darts to take out 161, and after missing double top, then double ten, he nailed double ten.

Wife Sarah, having sobbed and screamed her way through 133 minutes of seesaw drama, climbed on stage to squeeze her hero.

"It was more for my wife than it was for me," said Hankey. "My world had fallen apart and without Sarah I would probably be dead. That's why winning that world title meant so much."

O'Shea remembered, "Even though I lost, it's still one of my favourite matches," and Wayne Baker, reporting on the championship for *Darts World* wrote: "In 29 years of covering this championship the clash certainly ranks in the top six matches."

Phil Taylor v James Wade

NO. 23   2008 World Matchplay final

YOU know how some people like to go to the same place every summer and do the same thing…

Phil Taylor was like that.

For years, he went to Blackpool every summer and won the World Matchplay.

Such was his dominance there – and just about everywhere else – the pre-tournament debates weren't about who would win the trophy, but rather, who would finish runner-up behind Taylor?

This went on for years, but in 2007, everyone fancied their chances against him.

For the first time since the PDC was formed, Taylor failed to win four successive televised tournaments – and the nadir came in Dublin.

Anyone who chooses 13 as their lucky number – Taylor was born in ward 13, brought up at 13, Boothfield Street – isn't going to have too many crises of confidence, but a first-round loss to Adrian Gray in the World Grand Prix left him wondering if he would ever be the same again.

"I was starting to think I couldn't beat these kids any more," he would say later. "I felt humiliated. I was losing and people were chanting: 'Easy, easy.'"

If Taylor wasn't going to dominate darts any more, James Wade looked sure to benefit more than anyone else…

2007 was his year.

Wade, a bespectacled, fluent left-hander, won the World Matchplay and World Grand Prix and he made a good start to 2008 as well, ending Taylor's 44-match unbeaten run in the Premier League.

An 8-3 loss to Peter Manley in Coventry a few weeks later brought Taylor to a crossroads in his career.

One road pointed towards further ridicule and possible retirement, the other offered a steep climb back to the top…

Ever the competitor, Taylor decided to "get on the treadmill, get on the practice board and do something about it".

He powered to the Premier League title, beating Wade in the final to avenge that loss on the opening week, then threw both a nine-darter and the highest televised three-dart average (114.53) at the UK Open and followed that by winning the Las Vegas Desert Classic.

By the time the World Matchplay got under way in July, Taylor and Wade were unquestionably the best two players in the world and had shared the two previous major tournaments.

Wade won the UK Open after Raymond van Barneveld had nudged out Taylor 10-9 in the quarter-finals, then Taylor beat Wade in the final in Las Vegas.

It hadn't gone unnoticed that although Wade had won three major tournaments in the previous 12 months, he had never beaten Taylor on the way to lifting a trophy.

In the matches that mattered most – the three finals they had contested – Taylor had won.

The World Matchplay was the culmination of the season and, possibly, the rivalry between Taylor and Wade, fought out under the splendorous ceiling of the Winter Gardens in Blackpool.

The Victorian theatre appealed to Taylor – "I like the place, I like the building, it's inspiring," he said – and the record books showed it brought out the best in him.

In 2002, he had thrown the first nine-darter televised live on British television there and had won eight of the previous 14 World Matchplays going into the 2008 tournament.

Wade was the defending champion – he had beaten Terry Jenkins in the previous year's final – and Sid Waddell, writing in the programme, said he recognised in Wade the same "inborn arrogance" that he had seen in Eric Bristow.

He added that Wade "will never lose his self-confidence... he's very naturally gifted but he's also got enormous arms and is pretty fit and strong... he has a really firm throw that may relax him in tight situations."

For all that, Taylor was the man to beat in Blackpool. Not only was he in form, but, behind the World Championship, the World Matchplay was the trophy he prized most and he would fight hard to get it back.

For five years, between 2000 and 2004, he was unbeaten at the Winter Gardens, but going into the 2008 event, he had lifted the trophy just once in the previous three years. In the opening round, he beat Steve Beaton – "a true Roman gladiator with plenty of hair wax", according to Waddell – and went on to wallop Colin Osborne, Kevin McDine and Dennis Priestley.

Taylor recorded skyscraping averages of 109.70, 95.78 and 105.59 respectively – and three times went close to a nine-darter on his way to the final.

Wade made his way through the bottom half of the draw with wins over Wayne Jones, Ronnie Baxter, Matt Clark and Wayne Mardle. His average against Mardle was 102.73, suggesting both finalists were at, or at the very least near, their peaks.

The expectation was of a classic final when Taylor and Wade duelled on a steamy Saturday night in front of Superman, Scooby Doo and more soberly dressed but equally high-spirited revellers.

They would see one of the sport's greatest ever legs – and possibly the best dart ever thrown...

The opening eight legs were shared as Taylor and Wade fought hard for control of the match.

Taylor levelled the match at 4-4 with a 121 checkout – his second ton-plus finish – and Wade matched it in the next to edge ahead 5-4.

Wade pulled away to lead 7-4, Taylor won the next three and the back-and-forth sharpshooting went on.

Wade took 12 darts to make it 8-7 and Taylor responded with legs of 13, 11 and 13 darts to lead 10-8.

The 19th leg went Taylor's way as well, against the darts, and Wade was showing signs he was hurt.

Even with an average of around 106, Wade, who had led the match 7-4, found himself 11-8 down. No wonder he shook his head.

It didn't get any better for him either. Wade didn't get a dart at a double in the next three legs as Taylor pulled away to lead 14-8.

"He could hit those trebles standing in a hammock – in a force nine gale," gushed Sid Waddell of Taylor during the 22nd leg – and better was to come...

Taylor stretched his lead to 16-8 and in the 25th leg, he didn't miss. Neither did Wade.

"We've never had a leg of darts like this before," gasped commentator Dave Lanning, who had seen most things in the sport in three decades behind a microphone.

Wade started with back-to-back 180s – and so did Taylor. For the first time Lanning, or anyone else, could remember, both players were on course for a nine-darter in the same leg after throwing six darts each.

Wade missed his eighth dart – at treble 19 – Taylor couldn't find a seventh treble 20 – and Wade went on to grab the leg in 11 darts.

Taylor was one leg away from the title after winning the next and wrapped up the match with a dart that made jaws drop.

Left 132, Taylor's first dart landed in the outer bull's-eye and treble 19 left him the bull's-eye. It looked an impossible shot, beyond even the finest of all darts players.

The bull's-eye was blocked and to give himself even half a sight of his target, Taylor had to edge right across the oche.

He was almost on Blackpool beach – only a minor exaggeration – by the time he let go of his last dart, and somehow it landed in the middle of the bull's-eye.

That dart, described as the best he had seen in 33 years of watching darts by Waddell, provided the perfect exclamation mark to a win that had to rank among the most satisfying of Taylor's career.

Taylor sobbed, "I'm proud of myself," as he was handed the trophy for the ninth time following a victory that set another record.

His average of 109.47 was the highest recorded in a major final.

Wade could have been excused had he sobbed as well. He averaged 102.58 – and was still walloped 18-9.

John Lowe v Keith Deller

NO. 22   1984 World Matchplay quarter-finals

IF anyone was going to throw a nine-darter that day it was Keith Deller.

Backstage at the Fulcrum Centre in Slough, Deller was throwing maximum after maximum as he prepared to play John Lowe in the quarter-finals of the World Matchplay, described by sponsors MFI as "the richest prize in darts".

But nobody seemed to care.

Dave Lanning remembers there being "only about 200 people" in the venue on what he described as "a grey autumn afternoon" in Berkshire and while Lowe and Deller duelled, ITV chose to show highlights of Bob Anderson beating Jocky Wilson.

Lanning had sensed something remarkable would happen in Slough and made an investment at odds of 50/1 there would be a nine-dart leg during the most lucrative tournament on the busy professional darts circuit.

The prize for a player who could put together nine perfect darts was a massive £100,000 – and the sponsors would add £2,000 to their winnings if the cameras captured it.

Snooker, the decade's other boom sport, had seen perfection. Steve Davis made a maximum 147 break at the Lada Classic in Oldham in 1982, while on the oche, Jocky Wilson, the gap-toothed, volatile Scotsman, had come closest to darts' equivalent in a televised tournament.

Wilson twice threw seven perfect darts on his way to winning the World Championship in 1982 and the following year, he came even closer during his semi-final against Keith Deller. After back-to-back 180s, treble 20 and treble 15, he pushed his ninth dart just outside double 18.

Lowe wasn't a flamboyant thrower like Wilson or Bobby George.

All that concerned him was chiselling his way down from 501 as quickly as possible and with the minimum of fuss. His nicknames – 'Gentleman John' and 'Old Stoneface' – reflected his fully focused, unblinking approach on the oche. There were even rumours he would advertise eye drops on television.

Lowe, a motorbike-loving son of a Derbyshire miner, tells a funny story about how he started playing darts.

He was watching a match at The Butcher's Arms in Brimington, near Chesterfield, with fiancée Diana and remembered: "Suddenly a fellow in one of the teams rushes past us to the gents. The skipper looks at me and says: 'Take his throw, mate.' So I picked up the darts the fellow had been using and I threw 100. The fellow never came back to the oche."

Fact or fable, Lowe was on his way...

It took him three years to become the best player in his local and he was in the Parkhouse Hotel team in Danesmoor that won the prestigious Nodor Fours, a national team competition, in 1972.

1976 was his breakthrough year.

His nerve steadied and competitive spirit sharpened by playing money matches, Lowe helped Yorkshire win the Inter-County Championship and later that year he won the British Pentathlon and World Masters.

By the time the World Matchplay started in October 1984, Lowe, his composed, textbook throw now perfected, was one of darts' biggest names. He had won the World Championship in 1979, along with the World Masters twice.

Deller, of course, had also won the World Championship and threw like a world champion in the minutes before he met Lowe.

Lowe was less well prepared for the World Matchplay. He arrived in Slough having spent the previous few nights playing exhibitions in the Norwich area.

His friend John Carmichael, a darts fan who owned a local trophy shop, organised the events and Lowe stayed at the Marlborough Hotel, run by another friend, Eddie Harvey.

Harvey and Carmichael were a hospitable pair and it was way beyond midnight when Lowe headed back to his room on the last night of his stay.

He remembers – just about – going to bed at three o'clock in the morning, and just three hours later he set off on the 140-mile trip to Slough.

Jocky Wilson and Eric Bristow went out in the first round – beaten by Bob Anderson and Terry O'Dea respectively – while Lowe made it through to the tournament's second day by beating Nicky Virachkul 2-1.

Deller beat Welshman Peter Locke by the same margin and on Saturday, 13 October he met Lowe for a place in the semi-finals.

Going into the second leg of the fourth set, Lowe was in charge.

He was 2-1 up in sets and had taken the opening leg of the fourth set against the darts.

He started the second leg with 180 and while Deller replied with 59, Lowe stood at the back of the stage wondering what Lanning would be saying in commentary.

Lowe's fourth and fifth darts also found the treble 20, but they blocked his view of the bed. He thought about switching to treble 19, but decided there was room for another dart in the treble 20 – and there was. He steered his sixth dart alongside his fourth and fifth – and the perfect leg was still on.

Lowe was now 141 points away from the first televised nine-dart leg.

Deller responded with 100, but knew the leg was lost and his most important contribution was to ask for quiet from the crowd when Lowe prepared to throw his seventh dart.

Lowe had been preparing for this moment.

He said: "I always said to my good friend Barry Twomlow that if I found myself in this position, needing 141 with three darts left, I would go the John Lowe way: treble 17, treble 18, double 18.

"My reasoning was that I would be on the same side of the board for all three darts and I would just have to raise my eyesight a little after each throw."

That wasn't the Fred Reader way.

Reader, a 27-year-old panel beater and sprayer from Tonbridge in Kent, had thrown the first nine-dart leg recorded in an open competition when playing in the East Grinstead Open in February 1981.

He remembered: "After my second 180 I picked one of my opponent's darts off the floor and he simply said to me: 'Take your time.'" Reader coolly nailed treble 20, treble 15 and double 18.

"I didn't get the shakes or go slow with those three darts," he said. "They all went in so crisp it was as though they had magnets on them. I couldn't sleep that night. I was pacing the floor like a lunatic."

Rather than aiming his seventh dart at treble 20, Lowe threw at treble 17 and his dart found the middle.

He slotted his eighth dart into treble 18 and just as he had planned, shifted his sights a few centimetres to throw for double 18, £102,000 and a place in the history books.

"I always thought that if I got to that double 18, I would walk off stage, walk back in and throw," he said. "But I just went straight at it."

Lowe didn't give himself time to think about that ninth dart and what it meant.

He just threw it.

"I knew it was going to hit the target," he remembered. "I think my arm was in the air before the dart hit the double."

Lowe shook a lot of hands and looked a bit embarrassed by all the fuss while caller Freddie Williams boomed: "Ladies and gentlemen, history has been made here in Slough today."

Lowe described his achievement as "unreal" when quizzed by Jim Rosenthal on television afterwards and added: "I have been aiming at it for so many years.

"I've listened to all these people saying they have done it in practice many, many times and I was thinking: 'When's a fella going to do it on television?' I predicted it would be done and I was hoping like hell it would be me."

Lanning also predicted it would happen and Lowe's perfect nine darts earned him a £12,500 payout from the bookmakers.

Lanning remembered: "John walked off stage and when I went over to interview him he said: 'You've won more than me!'"

Lanning added: "It was a heart-stopping moment for me when he threw for that double 18.

"Because of the angle of the board, I couldn't see if the dart had gone in and waited until referee Fred Williams called it until I said anything.

"I was so relieved when we played the tape back and I heard my commentary.

"I knew it was a massive moment and I was praying I hadn't said anything stupid. I thought I had been very professional."

After the handshakes and backslapping, there was still a match for Lowe to win – and he won it.

He went on to whitewash Bob Anderson 4-0 in the last four – taking out a 161 finish that earned another £1,000 for the biggest checkout of the tournament – and came from behind to beat Cliff Lazarenko 5-3 in the final.

For winning the tournament, Lowe banked another £12,000 and that took his winnings to a staggering £115,000 for three days' work.

FOR years, if you were the best darts player in Stoke-on-Trent, you were the best darts player in the world.

Between them, 'The Power', 'Jackpot' and 'the Count' – or Phil Taylor, Adrian Lewis and Ted Hankey if you prefer – have won 20 World Championships at the time of writing and they grew up just a few miles apart in Burslem, Cross Heath and Bentilee respectively.

Lewis made it back-to-back World Championships in 2012 with victory over another neighbour, Andy Hamilton from Dresden, when Stoke met Stoke in the biggest darts match of them all.

Further back, Eric Bristow was based in the Potteries.

He shared a house with women's No. 1 Maureen Flowers in the village of Tean, next to the church, and he clearly enjoyed the surroundings.

Bristow won four of his five world titles in Stoke – the BDO World Championship was held at Jollees Cabaret Club underneath the bus station in Longton between 1978 and 1985 before moving to the Lakeside Country Club in Frimley Green – and he opened 'The Crafty Cockney' pub there in 1983.

Pubs are important in working-class communities like those found in Stoke. Historically, workers there earn among the lowest wages in the country.

For them, the Twenties didn't roar and the Sixties never swung. They just tried to get by the best they could.

The hardship brings people together, to the pub, where grievances are aired, life's struggles forgotten for a night and darts thrown.

Plenty of darts were thrown at The Saggar Makers Arms, the Great Eastern Working Men's Club and The Cockney.

Bristow would serve behind the bar at the latter, play exhibitions and the pub, now The Moorland Inn, also became Staffordshire's home venue for county fixtures.

Taylor also played for Staffordshire and for several years the women's team included Yvonne Lewis.

But she had to give up playing darts when she became pregnant.

Her son, Adrian Lewis, was born in January 1985 and although he remembers throwing his first darts at the family home in Cross

Heath when he was just five years old, his boyhood passion was football.

Lewis went to watch Stoke City with his grandfather and as a teenager was a goalkeeper on the books of Crewe Alexandra. His football ambitions were dented by a hand injury suffered in a street skirmish after Lewis came to the rescue of a friend and he started to play more darts.

Aged 18, he won the British Teenage Open in 2003 and the following year set about qualifying for the PDC's UK Open. At the time, Lewis was working as a builder and needed a day off work to play in a crucial qualifying event.

Lewis remembered: "My boss said: 'Do you want to pay the bills or play darts for fun?' He told me if I didn't turn up for work on Saturday, I shouldn't bother turning up for work again. I took the gamble."

The gamble paid off.

Lewis qualified for the UK Open and a few weeks later he met Taylor while playing in the Staffordshire Super League at Maureen Flowers' pub, The Sneyd Arms in Tunstall.

"Phil had already heard about me," remembered Lewis, "and asked if I wanted to practise with him at his mum's house in Burslem.

"We practised for a couple of hours every day and Phil was brilliant. He was constantly throwing nine-darters and beating me up. After five or six months of that I turned up one day thinking 'I'm going to have you today' and I beat him.

"I qualified for three televised tournaments before I met him, but Phil helped me a lot with my maths because that wasn't my strong point. He taught me a lot."

Lewis was perhaps too grateful.

When they met on the big stage, there was only ever one winner in matches dubbed "bun fight at the oatcake Corral" by commentator Sid Waddell.

By the time they met in the semi-finals of the World Grand Prix in October 2010, Lewis had shown he could beat anyone in front of the television cameras – apart from Taylor. He had lost all 14 previous meetings between them in major tournaments.

Lewis would later admit he felt intimidated by Taylor's achievements and it showed. Faced with Taylor, his throwing lacked its usual fluency and fire and among those defeats were some thrashings.

There was an 11-1 pasting in the Premier League semi-finals in 2009 and a whitewash in the final of the German Darts Classic a few months later.

Taylor was thrashing everyone in 2010. Before Dublin, he had won the World Championship, Premier League, UK Open and World Matchplay – and for all his brilliance, not everyone enjoyed watching it.

Lewis remembers a fan telling him before he played Taylor in Dublin: "If you don't win tonight I'm never watching darts again."

Before the World Grand Prix, Lewis had made the decision to stop practising with Taylor. "Phil understood," he said. "I'm an aggressive player, but didn't have the bit between my teeth enough when I played Phil. He was my mate."

The double-in format at the World Grand Prix – players had to start and finish legs on a double – had given Taylor problems in the past. He had lost in the first round three times – to Kevin Painter, Andy Callaby and Adrian Gray – but every time he cleared the opening hurdle, 'The Power' went on to lift the trophy.

To stop him lifting it for the tenth time, Lewis said he had to win the opening set of their semi-final.

He did just that and went on to lead 2-1 in the best-of-nine-sets match.

But Taylor won nine of the next 11 legs to go ahead 4-2 and that left him needing just one more set.

Something happened at the end of the sixth set that changed the course of the match – and darts history.

"I remember seeing Phil dancing with the crowd when he was 4-2 up," said Lewis, "and I thought to myself: 'Come on Adie, it's about time you beat him.'"

The match with the Shakespearean subplot took another twist.

Lewis saved the match by winning the seventh set with the help of a 121 checkout and three maximums and the crowd got behind him. In between throws, he conducted their chants. "Looo-is! Looo-is!" they thundered.

Throwing quicker now and not missing as much, Lewis talked to himself while he threw and whatever he was saying, it worked.

He broke Taylor's throw in the opening leg of the eighth set after firing in two more maximums, then flamboyantly finished 80 with two double tops in the next.

The crowd cheered the showman and Taylor started to feel the pressure.

He failed to find the starting double with his first three darts of the third leg and as he plucked his arrows from the board, Taylor clapped his hands and turned to look at Lewis.

This was possibly a response to some of Lewis's tactics. After the match, Taylor would e-mail a complaint to the PDC about Lewis "clicking his darts, stamping his feet, talking to himself when I was throwing."

Lewis seemed puzzled by Taylor's applause, but wasn't distracted.

He wrapped up the eighth set for 4-4 and had the advantage of the throw in the decisive ninth.

But his comeback looked like ending there.

Taylor ignored the crowd's boos to win the opening leg against the darts, then held his throw to move to the brink.

He had a dart at double top to win the match in the third leg, but missed after Lewis had cranked up the pressure with his 16th maximum.

Lewis clinched the leg, but still had to break Taylor's throw in the fourth to save the match.

Taylor missed a dart at the bull's-eye for the match and in a moment of heart-stopping do-or-die drama, Lewis, knowing another miss would surely cost him the match, desperately flung his final dart into double eight.

The crowd went loopy for Lewis and with them behind him, the final, deciding leg couldn't start soon enough.

Lewis had the throw and had chipped his target down to 344 before Taylor found his starting double top with his fifth dart.

Lewis didn't let Taylor back into the leg and wrapped up the match with a 106 checkout.

He was shaking when interviewed by Dave Clark on Sky Sports minutes later and, although beaten by James Wade in the final the following night, Lewis knew Taylor's grip on him was lost forever.

Three months later, Lewis looked back at his victory over Taylor after winning the PDC World Championship.

"I was probably 100/1 to win that match and I'm a different player since beating Phil," he said. "I know I can beat anyone now. That match was the turning point of my career."

Raymond van Barneveld
v Jelle Klaasen

JELLE Klaasen looked as out of place as a young, thin teetotaller at a World Darts Championship.

Which is what he was.

The more portly, avuncular Raymond van Barneveld looked rather more like a darts player – and some darts player he was too.

Four times in the previous eight years he had been crowned BDO world champion and if he won again, he would equal the record of BDO world titles won by Eric Bristow.

Van Barneveld admitted that thought brought pressure – and he had other troubles as well.

2005 had been something of an *annus horribilis* for the Dutchman. He admitted he "lost a lot of matches" and split with his manager, Ad Schoofs.

But unlike ex-champions John 'Boy' Walton, Andy Fordham and Ted Hankey, van Barneveld didn't lose in the first round of the BDO World Championship.

He didn't convince either. His average was just 85.83 in his 3-0 win over Danish qualifier Brian Sorensen and van Barneveld was awful, admitting afterwards that his "finishing was unbelievably bad".

The best match of the first round was between Peterborough panel beater Dennis Harbour and Klaasen, a 21-year-old qualifier from Alphen in southern Holland.

Harbour went 2-0 up in the best-of-five-sets match and remembered: "I thought I was going to win, then all of a sudden he started taking out ton-plus finishes. He just went up a gear. He was a fast thrower and I felt a bit rushed.

"I didn't feel I could play at my own pace. He was hitting everything, the crowd got behind him and I started thinking the world was against me."

Klaasen, just a treble 19 and double 12 away from a nine-darter in the third set, went through 3-2 and watching every twist and turn – mostly through the gaps in her fingers – was Yvanca van Welt, his girlfriend.

She had encouraged Klaasen to turn what he described as "an addiction" into his job.

Klaasen had started playing darts in 2002 after an ankle injury ended his football ambitions.

"My uncle played darts for 15 years," he said, "and I watched him a few times and thought: 'That's a nice game, I might try it.'"

Klaasen found he was "not too bad, better than most of the guys, but in a few weeks I could beat my uncle."

He liked winning.

"I like to play pool, snooker, tennis," said Klaasen, "and every sport I play, I want to win. I think that's what's important: to be a winner."

By December 2005, he was winning enough money to give up his job as a security guard and become a professional darts player.

He went on to reach 'the Lakeside' at the first attempt by winning the qualifying tournament in Bridlington.

'The Matador' – "I always hit the bulls," he explained – arrived at the World Championships as a 100/1 outsider, throwing fast darts that hit the board hard.

"There was a TV interview with me and two other young Dutch players who had qualified," remembered Klaasen. "They both said they wanted to win their first game and I said I wanted to win the tournament. I thought I had a chance."

Klaasen said he admired players like Mervyn King and Ted Hankey, but added: "The Dutch guys: our maths is better, we calculate better, faster."

Better-looking too.

The tabloids lapped up tales of randy female fans posting underwear to Klaasen and wrote headlines like: "One Hunk-dred and Eighty".

He got more ink when Yvanca told the press she would propose to Klaasen on stage if he won the World Championship.

The result that really got typewriters tapping was Klaasen's second-round win over King, the No. 1 seed.

King said after losing 4-2: "If he keeps his head he will have a very good chance, but we will have to see if he can do that. The lad was brilliant against me."

Klaasen was also too good for Paul Hogan and in the semi-finals, Shaun Greatbatch, while in the other half of the draw, van Barneveld, so disappointing in the first round, upped his average in wins over Gary Anderson and Tony O'Shea.

By the time he met Martin Adams in the semi-finals, van Barneveld was throwing his best darts.

The match was a repeat of the previous year's final and the scoreline was the same, van Barneveld winning 6-2 after reeling off 12 straight legs to open up a 5-1 lead.

Van Barneveld–Klaasen would be the first world darts championship final of any description to be played out between two non-Britons and back home in Holland, a third of the 16 million population tuned in to watch on television.

As van Barneveld had hoped, Bristow was at the Lakeside Country Club and he knew that if Klaasen won the best-of-13-sets match, he would replace him as the youngest winner of the trophy at 21 years and 90 days.

"I said my chances were 50-50," remembered Klaasen, "and Raymond said that with the averages I had been throwing, I wouldn't beat him.

"There was no pressure on me."

Klaasen raced to the opening two sets inside 20 minutes.

It could have been 1-1, but van Barneveld found, as he had done at times throughout the tournament, the doubles seemed to shrink when he really needed to hit them and he missed twice.

Klaasen then started missing, van Barneveld found his rhythm and the next two sets went to the defending champion without reply. The fifth set should have gone van Barneveld's way as well, but he missed six darts at a double and Klaasen went 3-2 ahead instead.

Van Barneveld, sweaty and wistful, pulled himself together to win the sixth set against the darts and held in the seventh to go ahead for the first time in the match.

Klaasen tied the scores at 4-4 by winning the eighth without reply – and though van Barneveld had the throw in the ninth, Klaasen was in the middle of one of his purple patches.

As John Part said of Klaasen in commentary: "Sometimes he's on, sometimes he's off and when he's on, he's untouchable."

He needed only 12 darts to break van Barneveld's throw in the opening leg of the ninth set and went 5-4 up with a breezy 104 checkout that had the crowd chanting "Jelle! Jelle!"

Klaasen had the darts for 6-4, but with the match in his grasp, his scoring dipped and a match that had swung back and forth throughout swung back van Barneveld's way.

The scores were level at 5-5, but the advantage was with van Barneveld. If he held his throw in the 11th set, the pressure would be on Klaasen to hold in the next to save the match.

That 11th set went to a deciding leg after van Barneveld missed a dart at double 16 for 6-5.

Van Barneveld had the throw, outscored Klaasen, got to the double first – and missed. Four times. That gave Klaasen a chance, half a chance really. With 106 left, he had to find a treble to get one dart at a double.

Klaasen threw single 20, treble 18 and in the blink of an eye, he switched his sights across the board and nailed double 16.

The match was now Klaasen's to lose. He only had to hold his throw in the 12th set to become world champion, but given what had gone before in this most topsy-turvy of matches, there was always the chance he would blow cold for a few minutes, allowing van Barneveld to break and save the match.

The opening three legs of the 12th set went with the throw and in the fourth, Klaasen crept up on van Barneveld and fashioned a shot at 101 for the title with van Barneveld sitting on 52.

Again, Klaasen would only get one dart at a double – if he hit a treble.

He went for the bull's-eye with his first dart, hit 25 and without a moment's thought, stuck his next two darts in treble 20 and double eight and the match was won.

The place went mad and Klaasen made his way into the crowd to kiss Yvanca.

"I couldn't stay with him," shrugged van Barneveld, while an overwhelmed Klaasen spent post-match interviews prodding the trophy and mumbling one-word answers.

Viewers wondered if Klaasen was overwhelmed.

"I'm calm, that's the way I am," he explained years later. "I never get that excited. You never know what will happen in the future." There were no proposals of marriage and the romantics among those watching 12 months later noticed that when Klaasen returned to defend his title, he had a new girlfriend with him.

Jocky Wilson v Eric Bristow

1989 BDO World Championship final

IN retirement, Eric Bristow admitted the only players he ever feared were John Lowe and Jocky Wilson.

"John was the steady one," he said, "and Jocky was flamboyant.

"You never knew what he was going to do.

"Nobody could throw like Jocky.

"He would jump up in the air when he threw his last dart and you would think: 'Great, I'm going to get another shot.' Then you'd hear: 'Game, shot.' The dart will be in the middle of double top and you would think: 'How did that go in?'"

Only Wilson, a squat, toothless Scot, knew how he did it, but "seven or eight vodkas to keep my nerves in the proper state" seemed to help.

His favourite tipple was what he called "magic Coke"; that is, a litre bottle of Coca-Cola with half the Coca-Cola poured away and replaced by vodka.

John Thomas Wilson grew up on a council estate in Kirkcaldy on the east coast of Scotland and, in the days before he discovered booze and curry, he showed promise as a pole vaulter before leaving school at 14.

He drifted in and out of jobs – he was a miner and coal deliveryman – and first dabbled in darts aged 19 when he was roped in to play for his local pub team after someone didn't turn up.

Wilson was beaten before he had even found his starting double and, embarrassed, he put up a dartboard at home and started to practise as often as he could.

The more he practised, the better he got and in 1978 Wilson reached the semi-finals of the News of the World Individual Championship where he lost a match to Stefan Lord he really should have won.

The following year, Wilson made his debut at the BDO World Championship – and that was where Sid Waddell first saw him.

Waddell remembered: "This lad with a horrible shaggy mullet walked into the bar wearing a ragged old anorak, with a cheese sandwich poking out of one of the pockets, and carrying a suitcase the size of a matchbox. Straight away, he challenged my co-

commentator, Tony Green, to a match with a fiver at stake, because he was skint and Jocky was playing away into the wee hours of the morning, blissfully oblivious to the fact he was supposed to be preparing for the biggest tournament of his life."

Wilson still reached the quarter-finals and won the World Championship in 1982, beating John Lowe 5-3 in the final.

During that match, Lowe remembers strange moments when Wilson turned to him after throwing 180s and asked: "Am I doing OK? Am I performing to a professional enough standard?"

Wilson was taking on the darts establishment – and he was winning.

Lowe admitted: "The thing was that as he polished off another set with an incredible checkout, he turned to me and kept winking in delight and it was impossible not to share his joy. He was such an infectious character."

Wilson was also recognisable.

He was 5ft 4ins tall, was known to weigh around 17 stones and had lost all his teeth. He described himself as "boozy, fat and toothless".

Nicknamed 'Gumsy' on the circuit, Wilson would claim his tooth loss was because he used to brush his teeth with Fanta, the fizzy drink. "My granny told me the English poisoned the water," he said.

In Bristow, he found his nemesis; a similarly irascible talent whose competitive fires matched his own.

Bristow remembered Wilson taking "four inches of skin off my leg" with a kick in the shins before a match and there were other ways to disrupt Bristow, reckoned Wilson. "Hide the bastard's fags," was his advice. Wilson had, in the words of Waddell, "all the psychology of a claymore. He breathes aggression on the oche."

Wilson was the No. 5 seed for the 1989 BDO World Championship and Bristow was No. 3. Bristow wasn't looking himself.

He had bottle blond streaks in his hair and, more importantly, what Waddell had called his "praying mantis" throw was no more. Dartitis had tightened its grip on Bristow.

He was taking around one and a half seconds longer to release each dart.

"I pull the dart back and it locks," said Bristow. "The problem is letting it go. I want to let it go and it's stuck in my hand."

How did it happen?

"I was trying to be too perfect," reckoned Bristow. "I should have just let it go. I wanted to be better than I was."

In the build-up to the World Championship, Bristow practised eight hours a day, but in his autobiography *The Crafty Cockney* he would admit: "Whereas before I'd put the dart wherever I wanted to put it in the dartboard, now I had to work to put it there.

"Before, when the dart left my hand, I knew where it was going. Now I felt as if I had to push it towards the target and I was never sure exactly where it would land.

"Prior to 1988, if I'd had three darts at double 16, anybody I played put their darts away because they knew it was over. Now they kept them out. They knew I was there to be had."

But he still reached his eighth World Championship final in ten years, beating No. 2 seed John Lowe 5-1 in the last four.

In the other semi-final, Wilson, taken to a deciding leg by Alan Warriner in the second round, put out defending champion Bob Anderson.

"I'm going to kill him," predicted Bristow with a smile before the best-of-11-sets final, "and he's going to kill me."

The opening five sets went to Wilson – he restricted Bristow to only four legs – and BBC presenter Tony Gubba wondered aloud to the watching millions at the interval: "Are we watching the public humiliation of Eric Bristow?"

Bristow headed to the players' bar, ordered a pint of lager and, spotting his sponsors looking "all doom and gloom", he told them: "Right, we'd better start playing now then. I've given him a head start."

Even at 5-0 down, Bristow was still Bristow.

"If anyone in the world can come back from this, it's Bristow," said commentator Tony Green – and he did.

Bristow won the sixth, seventh and eighth sets, but in the deciding leg of the ninth, Wilson had a dart at a double to win the match.

He was only a whisker away from double top, but should have been aiming at double 18.

With the World Championship a dart away, Wilson had miscounted and Bristow made the most of the reprieve to make it 5-4.

As the tenth set got under way, Waddell said: "If Jeffrey Archer had scripted this, people would have said it was far-fetched," and there was more drama to come…

In the fourth leg, Wilson missed double 18 for a 156 checkout and the match and, ever the gimlet-eyed predator, Bristow coolly polished off 130 on the bull's-eye.

For all the relief he must have felt, there were no celebrations from Bristow.

He matter-of-factly plucked his darts from the board, acknowledged Wilson's nod of approval and waited for the audience to settle so the fifth leg could get under way.

Wilson needed to hold to win the match, but Bristow broke him to force an 11th-set decider that, given the momentum he had, he would be fancied to win.

For six darts, they matched each other dart for dart and with the leg in the balance, Wilson threw a jerky 140.

This time, Bristow had no answer.

He went eight darts without finding a treble and that meant Wilson could afford to miss two more match-winning chances – his third and fourth – before finally flinging a dart into double ten.

The crowd were on their feet, Wilson sank to his knees.

He picked himself up to hug Bristow and jump around the stage punching the air.

For the next two years, Wilson was a quarter-finalist in the World Championship – losing to Mike Gregory and Kevin Kenny respectively – but in 1992 and 1993, he bowed out in the first round.

Wilson was never a force in the PDC and, away from the oche, he ran into problems.

He was ordered to pay his manager £30,000 following a dispute over his earnings and was declared bankrupt after being handed a large tax bill.

Beset by health problems, Wilson, who drank and smoked heavily throughout his adult life, moved with wife Malvina to a tiny council flat in Kirkcaldy that he seldom left for the rest of his life.

Wilson refused all interviews, but did open his door to Waddell.

He revealed that in Wilson's living room stood a large photograph taken after he had won the World Championship in 1982.

Wilson said he still watched darts on television. "I love screaming at those bastards I never got on with," he told Waddell.

He carried on screaming until his death in March 2012 at the age of 62.

"I was the first nutter of darts," said Bristow once, "and Jocky was the second."

ON a good night, Michael van Gerwen hoped to average around 110 and on a very good night, he could get to 115.

Phil 'The Power' Taylor had talked of one day reaching a magical, unbeatable 120 and until this night in Aberdeen, he had come closer than anyone.

His 118.66 against Kevin Painter in the UK Open in 2010 was the best seen in a televised tournament.

If anyone was ever going to better that, it was surely van Gerwen.

Once into his rat-a-tat rhythm, van Gerwen, one of sport's most recognisable talents with his bald head, green shirt and funny faces, hardly missed.

He won just about everything in 2015 and confidence was high.

"Most of the time, 98 per cent of the time, I feel unbeatable," he said.

He started 2016 by winning the Masters, then set about defending the Premier League title.

On the opening night in Leeds, van Gerwen was beaten by James Wade and following that loss, he seemed to redouble his efforts.

In his next two matches, van Gerwen blew away world champion Gary Anderson and Adrian Lewis.

Michael Smith was next.

Smith, from the darting hotbed of St Helens and looking how you might expect a darts player to look, endured a difficult start to his first Premier League campaign.

After three weeks, he had only one point from four games – he played twice on the opening night after Anderson was ruled out through illness – and his tournament average was around 88, 20 points less than van Gerwen's.

There were signs Smith's form was returning, however.

Smith, a former PDC under-21 world champion and conqueror of Taylor at the World Championships, had reportedly averaged around 130 in the UK Open qualifiers the previous weekend.

The Aberdeen crowd – 4,000 of them – didn't really care about van Gerwen and Smith or what sort of form they were in.

They had come to see Scots Gary Anderson, Robert Thornton and Peter Wright – and maybe have a drink or two as well.

Van Gerwen is the sort of player who empties bars – and at a darts match, that takes some doing.

But then, he is a special sort of sportsman. The sort who can take your breath away.

Smith knew all that. He was part of the busy PDC circuit van Gerwen had terrorised for a year or more. The 26-year-old Dutchman was the most feared darts player since Taylor was hoovering up titles in his pomp.

The first dart van Gerwen threw against Smith in Aberdeen landed just above the treble 20, but his next ten went pretty much where he wanted them to go and in no time at all he led 1-0.

Van Gerwen took 12 darts to win the next leg and scores of 140, 174 and 100 set up another 11-darter.

3-0 to van Gerwen and though Smith hadn't come close to a shot at a double, he wasn't doing much wrong, throwing maximum 180s in both the second and third legs.

Van Gerwen didn't seem to notice. He just kept doing what he was doing: that is, putting his first dart exactly where he wanted in the treble 20 and putting the next two pretty close to it.

He had found his range and rhythm and with every treble he hit, his confidence grew.

Van Gerwen was soon believing he couldn't miss – and as early as the fourth leg, Nigel Pearson, commentating for Sky Sports, mentioned a record average was possible.

That fourth leg was won with a jaw-dropping finish. Van Gerwen left 132 after nine darts and fired in bull's-eye, bull's-eye, double 16.

Surely he couldn't keep this up?

He could. His next seven darts all found the treble 20 – "I have never seen anything like it in my life," gushed a disbelieving Rod Harrington – and though van Gerwen veered wide of treble 19 with his eighth throw, a ten-darter was good enough to keep him on course for the record average.

Van Gerwen won the sixth leg in ten darts as well after scores of 140, 180 and 145 landed him on 36, leaving his average an astonishing 137.28.

That meant the record would be broken – smashed, really – if van Gerwen won the seventh leg in 15 darts or less.

Given that he had won the previous six legs in 11, 12, 11, 12, 10 and 10 darts respectively, he seemed certain to do it.

Van Gerwen, incredibly off target only ten times in the opening six legs, knew he was on course for the record and perhaps that thought – surely the only thought he had during the match up to that point – distracted him.

Whatever the reason, he threw his lowest score of the match, just 80, in the seventh leg.

His aim was soon corrected and after 12 darts, he had left 36.

If he found double 18 with his first dart, van Gerwen would end the match with a staggering three-dart average of 136.

Agonisingly, he was just outside double 18 with his first dart – and again with his second.

Van Gerwen adjusted his sights – too much. The last dart was dragged into 18 and from nowhere Smith, who everyone had forgotten about, came up with a 116 checkout.

Smith had avoided the humiliation of a whitewash – some achievement given the way van Gerwen had pummelled him from the opening throw of the match – and allowed himself a smile.

More importantly for everyone apart from Smith, van Gerwen was still on course for the record.

He went into the eighth leg with an average of 129.22 and scores of 100, 134, 83 and 134 left him 50 after 12 darts – and the record was on.

At that point, van Gerwen's nerve failed him. He took aim at 18 to leave 32 – a task not beyond a member of the Dog and Duck's B team – and hit one. He put his next dart in 17, then missed double 16.

Van Gerwen came back for another shot at the double – and this time, he needed only one dart to find his target, ensuring he finished the match with an average of 123.40, breaking the record set by Taylor six years earlier.

Van Gerwen expects a lot of himself, but even he had to be pleased with that.

He was even pleased he missed the chance to finish with a 136 average.

He said: "If I had hit that double 18 [in the seventh leg], that would have been the end of the road for me.

"I would never have had a chance to break my own record!"

Phil Taylor v Andy Callaby

2004 World Grand Prix first round

TO bet on Andy Callaby you either had to be crazy or Andy Callaby.

Put him in a line-up and the chances are you wouldn't pick out Callaby as a darts player. Standing alongside Andy Fordham and Peter Manley, he looked like a dieting pipe cleaner.

What really set Callaby apart from his peers was what he had between his ears.

Unlike just about every other darts player on the planet, he really did think he could beat Phil Taylor and he got his chance when they were drawn against each other in the first round of the World Grand Prix in 2004.

"I wasn't bothered by the draw when it was made," said Callaby. "Taylor was in great form and I was playing terrible. But it was in the first round over the best of three sets and I thought that was the best time to play him. You do get chances early on against Phil. They are not easy, but you do get them and if you take them, you've got a chance."

The way Callaby saw it, all he had to do was win six legs quicker than Taylor and if he threw his best darts for 20 minutes or so and Taylor missed a few, that was possible. "Phil is only the best because he can throw his best darts for two hours at a time whereas the rest of us can only do it for short periods," reasoned Callaby later. "That's why I fancied my chances."

Perhaps Callaby was right. Maybe the best-of-three-sets, double-to-start format did make Taylor vulnerable, but in five previous World Grand Prix tournaments, only Kevin Painter had beaten him.

Three years earlier, Painter came from behind to beat him 2-1 in the first round and, while it was a massive shock, 'The Artist' did have form having twice reached the quarter-final of the BDO World Championship.

Callaby had form himself – and most of it was bad.

He did reach the semi-finals of the Sheppey Darts Classic, but the 39-year-old painter and decorator from Wisbech headed to Dublin having suffered four successive first-round exits in PDC events.

The World Grand Prix was more to his liking, however. Unlike every other tournament on the circuit, players had to start every leg with a double – it was double-in in Dublin – and Callaby said: "I was brought up on double-to-start and that was to my advantage. It's a totally different game."

Callaby had only been a member of the PDC for a few months when he nudged out Wes Newton 4-3 in the final qualifier for the Grand Prix – but he had 25 years of darts experience.

Aged 14, he started throwing with his father Stephen at the Princess Victoria in Walpole St Andrew and within a few months, he was in the pub's team.

Callaby went on to play for Essex and Cambridgeshire and the backing of local snooker club Room at the Top in March, just a few miles from his Wisbech home, enabled him to give up his job and join the PDC in 2004.

The Room at the Top paid his entry fees and travelling expenses in exchange for a share of the winnings and for a few months those winnings didn't amount to much.

All the early exits left Callaby 106th in the world rankings – 105 places below Taylor.

'The Power' had won his 11th World Championship earlier that year by outlasting Kevin Painter in a gruelling, back-and-forth thriller that went all the way to a sudden death final leg and when he had recovered from that and reversed his decision to retire, he picked up the World Matchplay and Desert Classic titles.

Taylor was as close to invincible as it's possible to be and with the exception of his performances in the qualifiers, Callaby had been throwing Dog and Duck darts.

It looked a mismatch. The bookmakers took bets on Taylor not dropping a leg and lengthened their odds on Callaby winning the tournament to 2,000/1 after the first-round draw was made.

Callaby was more positive about his chances going into the match at the Citywest Hotel. "There are players who are beaten before they even start against Phil," he said, "but I wasn't like that. I saw it as a great opportunity. There weren't any nerves. I wasn't under any pressure. I had nothing to lose.

"I'm sure people do get intimidated playing him and I can understand it when you think about everything he has done. But it was my first year on the tour, so I hadn't seen him thrashing people week in, week out and maybe that helped."

Instead, the nervy start came from Taylor...

Both players wore green shirts – Callaby's was a size or two smaller than Taylor's – and in the opening leg, it took Taylor until his fifth dart to get under way by hitting a double. Despite that, he still won the first leg. 1-0 to Taylor.

In blood-splattered combat gyms, they call these moments 'fight or flight'. Either Callaby stood up to Taylor – or he caved in. Most cave in, but Callaby fought back and a 108 checkout levelled the match.

Taylor held his throw in the third leg, but couldn't shake Callaby off and the opening set went to a deciding fifth leg. Taylor had the throw, but Callaby matched him treble for treble and after 'The Power' failed to take out 141 and 52, Callaby nailed double eight to claim the opening set.

"I really fancied my chances after winning the first set," he said. "I had the throw in the second set and knew if I got off quickly he would feel the pressure."

Callaby threw fast, edgy darts and snarled his curled-lip disapproval at any that landed anywhere other than where they were aimed. Mostly, his darts went where he wanted them to. Throws of 140 and 180 left him 72 and he held his nerve to take out double top with Taylor waiting on 94.

Taylor had the darts in the second leg, but could only start with 40 and Callaby's 152 put him in charge. He got to the double first, coolly took out 67 and that meant if he held his throw in the next leg, the biggest scalp in darts would be his.

Both left big finishes in the third leg of the second set. Taylor chiselled his way down to 120, but before he could take aim at that, Callaby had a shot at 145.

It was a tough finish, taking him zig-zagging up and down and across the board, but each dart found its target; treble 20, followed by treble 19 and finally, incredibly, double 14.

Taylor had been beaten by the world No. 106. Unthinkable.

How did he do it?

"I scored steadily and went straight out when I got a chance," said Callaby simply, years later.

The PDC website screamed that night: 'Super Cally in Biggest Shock of All Time' – and Callaby afterwards told reporters: "I knew I could win tonight even if no one else did. The 145 finish wasn't too shabby was it?" Callaby wasn't finished there, either. "I don't fear anybody now," he said. "I've just beaten the best player there has ever been, so why should I?"

Callaby was through to the second round – but still had to pack his bags the following morning. "I don't know if my management only booked me in for one night," he said, "but I had to find a new hotel the next day…"

Callaby went on to scalp another former world champion, Dennis Priestley, in the second round before bowing out to Alan Warriner in the quarter-finals.

The Room at the Top threw a surprise party to celebrate when Callaby returned home – "My manager said there were a few sponsors who wanted to meet me and when I walked in, everyone was there wanting to shake my hand and buy me a drink" – and although he went on to reach the second round of the Las Vegas Desert Classic and beat John Part on his way to the quarter-finals of the UK Open in 2006, the good times didn't last.

His sponsors pulled out and Callaby said: "Unless you've got a sponsor, it's so hard to play on the darts circuit. It's like banging your head against a brick wall. I carried on paying my own travelling fees and expenses for a while, but it was too much…"

Callaby packed away his darts and went back to work. "People still stop me to talk about the match and tell me they won money betting on me," he said in May 2013.

Martin Adams v
Michael van Gerwen

2006 World Masters final

MICHAEL van Gerwen was 13 years old when he threw his first dart at a friend's house in Boxtel in the Netherlands.

"I was always fast," he said. "Right from the start. It was natural. I just want to find my rhythm."

More often than not, van Gerwen found, his darts landed where he wanted them to.

"When I'm playing well," he would say years later, "I just look at the board and they go in."

Aged 14, he threw a 13-dart leg against Wayne Mardle in an exhibition match and told him afterwards: "You will hear a lot of me."

Van Gerwen looked a tremendous prospect, but then again, so had Paul Wade.

Before he reached his teens, Wade had beaten Leighton Rees, Dave Whitcombe and been millimetres away from a match-winning double against Eric Bristow in front of 350 supporters at a pub near his Leicestershire home.

That was as good as it got for him...

The fire in his not inconsiderable belly went out after he broke his arm falling off his bike and at just 14, Wade was finished as a darts player.

Van Gerwen stuck at it.

He was 15 years old and had been throwing darts for only two years when he won his first major event, the Norway Open, in 2005.

The following year, friend Jelle Klaasen won the BDO World Championship with victory over Raymond van Barneveld to become the youngest-ever holder of either world title, but the rest of 2006 belonged to van Gerwen.

He won three gold medals at the WDF Europe Youth Cup, both the Northern Ireland and Welsh Opens, beat van Barneveld in the Bavaria World Darts Trophy before losing to Martin Adams in the last four and also reached the semi-finals of the BDO Grand Slam.

All of which meant the 17-year-old headed to Bridlington's Leisure World for the World Masters as the No. 3 seed – and the most talked about talent in darts.

The story was he was a natural and 'oh so fast', his whirring right arm machine-gunning darts into the board. Giles Smith would write of van Gerwen in *The Times* that he "has almost finished throwing his darts before he reaches the oche".

At 50, Adams was old enough to be van Gerwen's father; the Grand Old Man of BDO darts who would rather captain England than chase his fortune in the PDC.

'Wolfie' – his facial hair made him look like a wolf – was to darts what South London scoundrel Jimmy White was to snooker: an instantly recognisable talent whose nerve seemed to fail him when it mattered most.

Possibly his most memorable collapse came against Chris Mason in the quarter-finals of the 1999 World Championship and he had been trying and failing to win the World Masters since van Gerwen was wearing nappies.

Hit or miss, win or lose, Adams usually managed a throaty chuckle for the cameras and his gregarious personality helped keep him busy on the exhibition circuit, while van Gerwen fitted in his darts practice around his day job fitting bathroom tiles.

Van Gerwen made appeals for sponsors, but found nobody wanted to invest in his talent.

Continuing his good form, he reached the final in Bridlington and asked whether there would be any pre-match nerves against Adams, he answered decisively: "I'm never nervous."

Neither the bookmakers' odds, his opponent's reputation nor the crowd's loyalties bothered van Gerwen.

"He's got the bottle," agreed Bobby George, commentating on the match for the BBC. "He doesn't care. All he wants to do is play darts."

A few weeks earlier, Adams had beaten van Gerwen 6-4 in the Bavaria World Trophy and was also in form.

In the semi-finals, he thrashed Steve Farmer 6-0 with a 103.40 average and 61% success on his doubles, prompting commentator Tony Green to say he had never seen Adams throw better.

Adams didn't need to throw his best darts to open up a 4-1 lead in the best-of-13-sets final – each set was the best of three legs – as van Gerwen struggled to find any sort of rhythm.

That 4-1 lead should have become 5-1, but Adams couldn't hit double top with two darts and at 4-2 at the interval, van Gerwen was still in the match.

Adams moved further clear with a 124 checkout in the deciding leg of the seventh set, then started the eighth with a maximum and was expected to pull away. But he couldn't shake off van Gerwen and the Dutchman went on to win the set with a 104 checkout for 5-3.

Adams held his throw in the opening leg of the ninth set and van Gerwen started the next with what commentator John Part called "one of the fastest 180s I've ever seen".

Mouth hanging open – "Good job there's no flies around," quipped Green – he kept throwing fast, kept finding the target and after Adams failed to finish either 121 or 160 for a 6-3 lead, van Gerwen grabbed the set against the throw to trim the deficit to a single set at 5-4.

The pressure was now on Adams.

For all the talk of his experience being decisive, all he had really shown in 17 previous World Masters was that he didn't know how to win big matches, while at just 17 years old, van Gerwen had fewer scars, if any, and never seemed to be in any doubt that he would win.

Going into the tenth set, van Gerwen had the throw and, just as importantly, the momentum. "Everything's going in," said Part in commentary and in a flash, Adams' lead had been wiped out and the match was level at 5-5.

Van Gerwen won the opening leg of the 11th set with a 121 checkout to lead the match for the first time, but Adams broke straight back and with the throw in the deciding leg, he was the favourite for the set and a 6-5 lead.

But, left six darts to take out 81 with van Gerwen back on 204, Adams couldn't finish.

He missed six darts at doubles and van Gerwen snatched the set to edge ahead.

Amid the cheers and chatter of disbelief, Adams tried to gather his thoughts. He took a deep breath and said a few words to himself before the start of a 12th set he had to win to stay in the match.

Adams won the opening leg with a 161 checkout, but, given more time to think about the smaller finishes he really ought to take out and the importance of them, Adams twitched and missed.

He couldn't take out 77 in six darts to level the match at 6-6, allowing van Gerwen to squeeze in a set-saving double ten with his last dart.

Van Gerwen threw for the match in the third leg, started with 137 and this time, Adams didn't go with him.

He couldn't find a treble with his opening six darts and van Gerwen went on to win the match with a 99 checkout on double 18.

From 5-2 down, van Gerwen had won five straight sets to win the World Matchplay and at the age of 17 years, 174 days, rubbed Eric Bristow out of the record books as the youngest winner of a major ranking event.

Leighton Rees v Alan Evans

1978 BDO World Championship quarter-final

DID you notice the opening word was in capitals? It's meant to grab your attention and it must have worked if you've got this far.

In the 1970s, the BBC were looking for ways to grab the attention of viewers and, asked by his bosses to find "another snooker", Nick Hunter, an executive sports producer, suggested darts.

Hunter had been enthralled by darts ever since following Tony Barrett for a television documentary 15 years earlier. He loved the tension, the human drama and encouraging viewing figures for the Evo-Stik Golden Darts, Ladbrokes Matchplay and Butlin's Masters when they were screened on regional ITV stations, suggesting his interest was shared by a wider audience.

Once he was given the all-clear by the BBC, Hunter contacted BDO secretary Olly Croft to suggest a World Darts Championship…

Televised darts really started in 1972.

The Indoor League gave us darts – and other pub pursuits such as bar skittles – and London Weekend Television screened the finals of the News of the World Individual Championship from Alexandra Palace.

Seven million viewers and 12,000 fans in attendance – many of them Welshmen brandishing leeks in support of Alan Evans – saw Brian Netherton beat Evans in the final.

Netherton lifted the trophy, but Evans stole the show. He wore a red shirt, Cuban heels and a snarl and punched the air and jumped for joy when his darts found the doubles.

Evans had started throwing darts at his father's pub when he was still a toddler and dedicated more time to the game after rheumatic fever ended his hopes of playing football for Cardiff City when he was a teenager. The word from the Valleys was that 'Evans the Arrow' was flashy, full of himself and could really throw after sinking five or six pints of lager to steady his nerves.

Sid Waddell would write of Evans "… he promises, he sneers, the lips purse and the eyes glint. When he's on form he is poetry."

Evans was on form in the CIU National Team finals in 1969. He took out 114 to win the tournament and threw a punch in triumph that hit his captain flush in the face and left him flat on his back!

On another, less bloody, occasion, Evans won a match at Ferndale Labour Club in the Rhondda on Boxing Day 1974 by finishing 330 in six darts, throwing 180 followed by three bull's-eyes.

Evans was fond of finishing on the bull's-eye and wherever he went, he flew the flag for Wales.

Often, he wore a badge that read: "I am proud to be a Welshman" – and Bob Anderson said of him: "Alan was only small, but he became a giant when he pulled a Wales shirt on."

Leighton Rees, raised in the village of Ynysybwl, near Pontypridd, was another proud Welshman.

When he left school at 15 years old, teachers who noticed Rees was more interested in the rugby union results than his education wrote that he was "good only for reading the sports pages of the *South Wales Echo*".

Rees instead found work at a local factory that specialised in making nuts and bolts and stayed there for 21 years.

He started playing darts with his workmates during lunch breaks, throwing darts made in the factory, then moved on to the pub where he developed what would be known as his 'cobra' throwing style.

As for his clothing, Rees chose a cardigan, reasoning it was "comfortable, loose fitting and had two broad pockets – one for your cigarettes, one for your darts".

Wearing his favourite cardigan, he won the Welsh News of the World Individual Championship in 1970, 1974 and 1976 and on a proud and dramatic night at Wembley in 1977, he won the World Cup for Wales after Cliff Lazarenko missed three darts to win it for England.

Rees and Evans were Welsh team-mates – and the best of friends.

As Phil Taylor and Dennis Priestley would do a decade or so later, they travelled to tournaments together and shared their winnings.

Both were entered in the inaugural World Darts Championship – but who else would play in the tournament set to start at the Heart of the Midlands Club in Nottingham on 6 February 1978?

John Lowe remembers Mike Watterson, a snooker promoter who got the backing of Imperial Tobacco for the championship, ringing him at two o'clock in the morning and asking him to "find 16 professionals".

"We haven't got 16 professionals."

"Well find them, make them up."

Between them, Watterson, Lowe and Croft found eight seeds and eight unseeded players.

Eric Bristow, crowned World Masters champion at the age of 21 a few weeks earlier, was the top seed, followed by Lowe and Rees.

Evans was the No. 5 seed and though troubled by foot and abdominal problems, he would be well prepared.

He practised for five hours every day in the countdown to the World Championship and Rees was also in good form heading to Nottingham.

Weeks before the tournament got under way, he reportedly threw nine maximum 180s during an exhibition in Birmingham.

Matches at the World Championship – for the only time as it turned out – would be played over legs rather than sets and there was a shock on the opening night.

Bristow was dumped out in the first round by Conrad Daniels, an American publican who threw with all the urgency of a tortoise wading through treacle.

Bristow blamed over-confidence. "I lost to an idiot," he told reporters.

In the best match of the first round, Evans beat left-hander Alan Glazier 6-4. Between them, they threw six maximum 180s in the ten legs played and that set up a quarter-final between Evans and Rees, again over the best of 11 legs.

Rees, who whitewashed Australian outsider Barry Atkinson in the first round, admitted years later: "I would have rather played someone else." Evans, he explained, was "my best friend".

Evans started the match with a maximum 180, soon added another and went on to win the opening leg in just 13 darts.

He needed just 13 more darts to make it 2-0, but as Waddell would write of Rees, "he's never as dangerous as when his opponent thinks he's down", and so it proved.

Evans threw for a 3-0 lead in the next, both had 180s and Rees snatched it in 17 darts, then held to level the match at 2-2.

The match was in the balance and Rees would later say, "I had to get in a good leg" in the fifth.

Evans started with 60, Rees replied with 137 and his next six darts landed within a millimetre or two of each other in the treble 20, leaving him on four after just nine darts.

Rees described double two as his "bogey", but still found it with his first dart to complete a ten-darter that Hunter described as "the arrows that made darts live up to all our expectations".

David Vine, commentating for the BBC, described the ten-darter as "a new world record for competition darts" and noticing Rees picking up his beer at the end of the leg, he added he was "well on the way to another record. That's his fifth pint."

Rees held his throw for 4-2, Evans took out 160 to stay in touch, but couldn't break in the eighth leg and at 5-3 ahead Rees was just a leg away from the semi-finals.

He won the match in style by nailing treble 20, treble 17 and bull's-eye with his tenth, 11th and 12th darts of the ninth leg – all in the middle – for a 161 checkout.

Evans shook his friend's hand after the match-winning bull's-eye went in and told him: "Go on and win it and don't forget I want half the money!"

Rees edged out Nicky Virachkul 8-7 with a 13-dart leg in the deciding leg of their semi-final, then beat John Lowe in the final – and happily handed over £1,500 to Evans.

Rees would later write of his quarter-final against Evans: "It is a match I am willing to be remembered by."

Phil Taylor v Gary Anderson

2015 PDC World Championship final

PHIL Taylor won his first World Championship in 1990 and a quarter of a century later, he was fancied to win his 17th.

Following a wretched start to 2014 that left him considering retirement, Taylor went on to win the World Matchplay and Grand Slam of Darts with skyscraping averages.

But for all his good form, at 54, Taylor seemed tired of darts at times during a topsy-turvy 12 months.

"There's no respect," he said after louts had jeered him during the World Grand Prix and Masters and he seemed to feel the darts world, for all he had given it, was possibly turning against him.

Ever the competitor, the fire in his belly returned and although Taylor still lost now and then, the defeats often weren't by much and were usually over the shorter distances.

The feeling was that if Taylor threw his best darts in the World Championship at Alexandra Palace over the longer distances, the others hadn't a hope and accordingly, the bookmakers made him the favourite, ahead of defending champion Michael van Gerwen and Adrian Lewis.

There were also those who fancied Gary Anderson's chances…

Anderson was as fluent as anyone, but on the big occasion, his nerve seemed to fail him.

He reached the World Championship final in 2011 – losing to Adrian Lewis – then won the Premier League a few months later, but following the death of both his brother Stuart and father Gordon in the space of six months, Anderson admitted he lost the desire to throw darts.

He says the birth of son Tai remotivated him. "When the wee one arrived," he said, "I pulled myself up."

By the time the 2015 PDC World Championship started, Anderson was the player in form having won seven PDC Pro Tour events during 2014 and beaten both Taylor and Lewis on his way to winning the Players Championship finals.

If only he could see what he was doing!

Anderson told the press following his first-round win over Scott Kirchner that he had a degenerative eye problem.

He said: "I can see the wide red and black segments of the board, sometimes the green. I can see the colours fine, but if I'm close to the wires, then it's a bit iffy.

"On the doubles, I can see the strip, but I can't see the wires. I have to rely on the ref shouting: 'Game!' and if he doesn't, I know I've missed it."

Anderson ruled out eye surgery, contact lenses and glasses and said he would carry on throwing until he couldn't see any more.

Taylor, beaten by PDC World Youth champion Michael Smith in a second-round shock 12 months earlier, had his troubles as well. His mother, Betty, had been taken ill and was in a care home when the World Championship got under way.

Taylor said darts had been his "sanctuary. I can forget everything and just play darts."

He threw them well enough to beat German Jyhan Artut, who had confidently predicted victory beforehand, then Mark Webster, Kim Huybrechts, Vincent van der Voort and Raymond van Barneveld.

Taylor came from behind to beat both Huybrechts and van der Voort, but never went a break behind in either and therefore, wasn't faced with any great crisis, just the sort of pressure he had been dealing with for the past quarter of a century.

Against van Barneveld in the semi-finals, Taylor was twice seven-ninths of the way towards a perfect leg and ended the match with a three-dart average of 102.39, his second best of the championship.

Anderson reached the final by beating Jelle Klaasen in one of the matches of the tournament, then Peter Wright, runner-up the previous year, and defending champion van Gerwen.

Van Gerwen had beaten Anderson in the third round on the way to winning the championship in 2014, there was needle between them and when it mattered in their semi-final 12 months later, van Gerwen missed and Anderson didn't.

The Dutchman missed four darts for a 4-3 lead, Anderson took his chance and pulled away to win.

Anderson had said, "If you're going to win a major tournament, you want to beat Phil. Even when he's playing his D or E game, he's still a tough man to beat."

Anderson got his wish in the World Championship final in front of a television audience of more than 1.7 million on *Sky Sports*, more viewers than golf's Ryder Cup or Test match cricket.

The tournament averages showed there wasn't much between Taylor and Anderson going into the final and Taylor knew he couldn't afford to give Anderson too many chances. In 17 attempts at double top in his semi-final against van Gerwen, Anderson found his target 14 times.

The bookmakers went for Taylor – if with not too much confidence – in the best-of-13-sets match and in the press room, they were soon predicting a long night…

Taylor gave away the advantage of the throw after winning the nearest the bull's-eye and although he couldn't get the early break he wanted, Anderson needed two maximum 180s and finishes of 120 and 121 to grab the opening set in the deciding leg.

The second set was just as keenly fought. There were five maximum 180s – Taylor threw three of them – and 'The Power' recovered from losing the first two legs to snatch the set at the fifth attempt after Anderson missed double ten for 2-0.

That was the sort of match it was turning out to be. There wasn't much between them.

The first break of throw went Anderson's way in the fourth set and at 3-1 ahead, he was in charge of the match.

If he held his throw, Anderson would be world champion.

But he couldn't hold his throw. Taylor won nine of the next ten legs to lead 4-3 and now he had the darts in the eighth set for a two-set advantage.

In the deciding leg of that eighth set, Taylor missed three darts at double 12 and Anderson nailed double eight with his do-or-die last dart for 4-4.

The ninth set was even more dramatic.

Anderson's first two darts found treble 20, but his third knocked the other two out of the board, leaving him with no score.

Ruthless as ever, Taylor stepped in with a maximum and went on to break.

Anderson had a chance to break back in the next leg, but at the moment he threw at the double, someone in the crowd whistled to distract him and he missed.

The set was surely Taylor's now…

Not only was Anderson 2-0 down and needing two breaks, but everything seemed to be against him as well.

Anderson, it seemed, was incapable of a negative thought, however. He remembers thinking: "This would be some set to win from here!"

Somehow, Anderson did snatch the set after Taylor missed three darts for a 5-4 lead.

The commentators claimed the set was one of the finest ever seen at the World Championship – and no wonder.

Anderson had taken everything Taylor, Lady Luck and the crowd could throw at him and fought back magnificently to edge ahead 5-4.

Taylor had the throw in the tenth set and started it with a 12-darter, wrapped up by a 103 checkout, but, as he had done throughout the match, Anderson found a response.

He won the second leg after starting with six treble 20s, then got the all-important break in the third leg and took out 98 for a 6-4 lead, leaving him just one set away from the match.

If Anderson held his throw in the 11th set, he would win – but Taylor started it with eight perfect darts.

He missed double 12 for the nine-darter, but more importantly, got the break he needed and went on to win the set without reply to trim the gap to 6-5.

The 12th set went to a deciding leg and after Anderson didn't get anywhere near a 170 checkout for the match, Taylor took his chance to send the match to a deciding 13th set.

Taylor had thrown everything at Anderson in the 11th and 12th sets to wipe out his 6-4 lead and with the momentum behind him and all his big match experience, he was surely now the favourite.

"I had been there three or four times," said Taylor of the last-set decider, "and Gary hadn't."

Anderson held in the opening leg and while Taylor wasn't looking, he took control of what would prove to be the decisive second leg.

"Stand up if you love the darts," bellowed the crowd and Taylor raised his arms to them.

But while his back was turned, Anderson fired in another 180, his 19th of the match, to heap the pressure on Taylor.

This time, Taylor cracked.

He put three darts at double 16 on the wrong side of the wire and Anderson stuck his next one in the middle of double 18 for a break that left him throwing for the match.

With the tension at its peak, Anderson somehow started the third leg with another maximum 180 and went on to win one of the great World Championship finals by nailing double 12.

The stats showed that Taylor missed 55 attempts at doubles – including darts to win the eighth set for a 5-3 lead – and Anderson went on to outlast him over two and a half hours to win one of the great finals.

Phil Taylor v
Adrian Lewis

2013 World Matchplay final

PHIL Taylor had a way of getting to his opponents before matches.

He was nice to them.

"Phil says nice things about you and puts you in a comfort zone," said Dennis Priestley, "then he goes out and murders you."

Maybe it was a tactic – or maybe Taylor was just being nice.

Either way, nobody Taylor ever played got motivated by his pre-match putdowns.

The others, Peter Manley, Mervyn King, Paul Nicholson, picked the fights and one by one, Taylor saw them all off.

The odd defeat apart, he was too good for all of them.

If ever there was a sportsman who didn't have to cheat, it was Taylor.

For a couple of decades he was a dart ahead of his rivals – great players like Priestley, John Part and Raymond van Barneveld – and 2013 looked like it was going to be another good year.

Taylor won the World Championship – for a 16th time – UK Open and the Gibraltar Darts Trophy.

The latter success was tarnished by the double 12 that wasn't.

Footage showed that during his semi-final win over Dean Winstanley, Taylor claimed a leg after his dart landed a fraction outside the wire.

The mistake went unnoticed by referee Russ Bray and Taylor himself and when film of the incident emerged on the internet, Taylor apologised and offered to either replay or forfeit the game.

As he said himself, Taylor was "never a cheat" and to his surprise, Eric Bristow didn't seem so sure.

He told the national press: "The player knows if it's not in and has to declare it. You don't want cheats."

Though he liked to provoke, Bristow was usually loyal to "Tay-lah". When others doubted him, Bristow remained an ally, but on this occasion, Bristow turned on him.

Taylor would admit 'Double Twelve Gate' made a hard tournament harder, but Taylor being Taylor, he was up for the challenge of winning another World Matchplay, a month before his 53rd birthday.

He liked playing darts in Blackpool. He had won the previous five World Matchplays there – and 13 in total. Taylor extended his unbeaten run on his favourite Winter Gardens stage to 32 matches with wins over Stuart Kellett (10-1), Terry Jenkins (14-12), Justin Pipe (16-10) and James Wade (17-12), upping his average in every match.

Against Wade, he recorded a mighty, just about unbeatable 107.61 – and the likelihood was, he would raise his average even higher in the final.

That didn't appear to bother Adrian Lewis. He had put a difficult spell behind him to win the European Championship earlier that month and in Blackpool, he showed something like his best form in back-from-the-brink wins over Andy Hamilton in the quarter-finals, then Michael van Gerwen in the last four.

In moody interviews, Lewis told Sky Sports ahead of the final with Taylor: "I know if I play my game I will win."

Lewis did go 6-4 ahead, then found himself 10-6 down as Taylor roared back, taking out finishes of 130 and 123 during a run of six successive legs.

Such was the quality of Taylor's throwing, several times Lewis applauded his marksmanship.

But when it seemed the match may get beyond him, Lewis found what he calls "his groove" – and the trebles started flying in.

In each of the eight legs between the 17th and 24th, Lewis threw a maximum 180.

But his aim was erratic.

Either he put all three darts in what Sid Waddell called "the red bit" or he threw none at all.

Such was his waywardness when he wasn't throwing 180s, Taylor still won four of those eight legs.

The 24th leg looked like being pivotal. Taylor won it against the throw to lead 14-10 and Lewis looked beaten. He gazed skywards and shrugged his shoulders.

Taylor held his throw in the 25th leg, then Lewis stayed in touch by winning a titanic, back-and-forth 26th that led Mardle to call the match "the best final in darting history in my opinion.

"The standard," he explained, "is the best ever."

There were three 180s and a 174 in that 26th leg and though Lewis nicked it after both missed chances, Taylor was still just three legs away from victory at 15-11 – and had the darts in the next leg.

Lewis knew it would take an almighty effort now to get back into the match and, despite soaring temperatures at the Winter Gardens, he produced it.

The sell-out crowd chanted: "Looo-is! Looo-is!" after he broke in the 27th leg to trim the gap to three legs at 15-12.

He wasn't beaten yet.

Lewis added the next with a 127 checkout on the bull's-eye and if he threw like that in the 29th leg as well, there was a chance he would break Taylor's throw again and cut the deficit to just a single leg at 15-14.

The crowd were behind Lewis and booed Taylor when he took aim at double 18, then double nine.

He missed, but despite the encouragement of the crowd, Lewis couldn't hit his doubles either.

Three times he missed.

Finally, Taylor nailed double one – not a double he's used to taking aim at – to lead 16-13 and went on to take out 136 for a 17-13 lead.

He held his throw in the 31st leg to lift the trophy again – despite two more maximums from Lewis that took his total for the match to a staggering 19.

Taylor threw nine and averaged 111.23, lifting his tournament average to 106.28, the best of his career.

"I've played in a few good finals," said Taylor, "but I think that was the best ever."

Lewis shrugged afterwards: "There will never be another Phil Taylor."

Phil Taylor v Eric Bristow

GEORGE Bristow told his son after the 1990 BDO World Championship final: "Don't teach anyone to do your job better than you."

In time, Eric Bristow would be proud of "the monster I created", but for months after that match, he couldn't bring himself to talk to Phil Taylor.

Bristow had taught Taylor everything he knew about darts – and by way of thanks, he had been humbled by his pupil.

Despite dartitis, Bristow reached the World Championship final again the following year – his tenth final in total – but was beaten by Dennis Priestley and following that defeat, he kept making early exits, until 1997 ...

Taylor was the defending champion, had won four world titles in total and was attempting to equal Bristow's record of five.

For all their similarities – they were ruthless in their pursuit of victory – Taylor and Bristow were also very different.

Taylor was the most grounded of sportsmen. He would clutch winner's cheques and say the money would pay the bills. He had bills to pay, just like everyone else, and he just happened to pay them by throwing darts better than anyone else. Taylor was humble and workmanlike. He behaved like David, but he threw like Goliath.

Bristow could never be so humble. He was the best – and wanted everyone to know it. He was the closest to Muhammad Ali darts would ever have and his outspokenness made him plenty of enemies.

"I don't need to be popular with the other players," he said once. "They don't pay my rent. As long as you're popular with your boss, that's all that matters. I'm my own boss – and I sleep well at night."

For a while he was Taylor's boss as well, having funded him at the start of his career, and millions of pounds and more than a dozen world titles later, Taylor would admit the debt he owed to Bristow for "teaching me how to win".

The fondness between them was mutual, but no matter how much he thought of Taylor, Bristow never threw darts to lose and would do whatever it took to win.

"He's a nasty piece of work up there," said Taylor, but when they met in the semi-finals of the WDC World Championship in 1997, Bristow's antics would backfire on him…

Bristow remembered in his autobiography that, going into the World Championship, the yips (his dartitis) had gone.

"They'd been on and off in the run-up to it – I'd have two weeks with them and two weeks without – but for the period of the championship there was no sign of them. The old Bristow was back…"

Back and throwing well enough to beat the No. 3 and No. 6 seeds, Bob Anderson and Alan Warriner respectively, to reach the last four and leave commentator Dave Lanning gushing: "It takes your breath away to see the resuscitation of a legend."

Taylor dropped only one set on the way to the semi-finals – where Bristow was waiting for him.

Bristow himself said years later: "If I was a darts fan and knew Eric Bristow was playing Phil Taylor, I would watch it. Something special might happen."

Most of the fans watching were rooting for Bristow.

Taylor remembered in his autobiography: "I could see before a dart was thrown for real that his self-belief was high.

"He had been going round telling everybody that he was the only bloke in the tournament who could beat me.

"Even before we started I was shaking. I had never had a crowd so obviously against me."

Bristow didn't have to do anything to get the crowd on his side.

They were with him from the start of the best-of-nine-sets match, pumping their fists to the rhythms of 'London Calling' by The Clash and willing him to be a great player again for them one more time.

The more trebles and doubles Bristow hit, the louder they cheered. Together, they would beat Taylor.

But though he didn't brag and was never unpleasant, Taylor would prove to be just as tough as Bristow ever was. This was Taylor's job as well; he had mouths to feed and he hated losing just as much as Bristow did.

For eight sets, they found each other's wills unbreakable.

Taylor did break in the fourth set to leave Bristow, in the words of Sid Waddell, "looking like a shoeless centipede", but when Taylor had four chances to grab the fifth set for a 4-1 lead, he couldn't take them.

Bristow trimmed the gap to 3-2 – and he had the throw in the sixth set.

He nicked it in the deciding leg to level the match, then turned and raised his arms to the jubilant crowd.

Bristow says he also "gave him [Taylor] the evil eye. He started biting his flights and I thought he was going to go."

Taylor admitted: "He was putting me under a lot of pressure. He was a brilliant player, but there are thousands of brilliant players. There's something about Eric…"

Taylor responded to the pressure magnificently, romping to the seventh set without reply to edge ahead again and when he took out 126 in the third leg of the eighth set, he was one leg away from winning the match 5-3.

Moments later, he was 108 points away…

A ton left Taylor double four – and Bristow had to take out 141 to save the match.

Waddell reckoned he wasn't throwing well enough to do it – but he was wrong.

Bristow smoothly picked off treble 20, treble 19 and double 12 and how the crowd cheered.

Taylor offered his right hand for a 'high five' gesture, Bristow slapped it hard and screamed: "Yeeeeahh!" in his face.

Bristow sensed those three darts may change the course of the match and they did, but not in the way he hoped.

Taylor said: "He slapped my hand so hard I thought: 'Right, I'm going to get you.'

"That was the turning point because I was gone. But my mindset changed after that."

The refocused Taylor couldn't prevent Bristow holding in the next leg to send the match into the deciding ninth set – and admitted he was feeling the pressure.

Taylor remembered: "I had two heartbeats, my heart was beating so fast. I was nervous, but I wasn't going to show him."

Or a crowd who thundered: "There's only one Eric Bristow!" and to their delight, Bristow jigged across the stage and sang along with them. In contrast, there had been barely a ripple of applause when Taylor polished off his finishes.

Taylor had the darts in the deciding ninth set that had to be won by two clear legs. If they were tied at 5-5 after ten legs, there would be a sudden death leg to determine who would go through to the final.

Bristow had a chance to break in the third leg, but missed double six and Taylor puffed out his cheeks in relief after he found the winning double.

Bristow held in the fourth leg to send the match into a tiebreak.

Taylor noticed Bristow "snatching the darts and going off balance" – a sign he was struggling – but still there were no breaks.

Taylor would hold his throw, then Bristow would hold his.

In the eighth leg, Taylor fashioned the chance of a match-winning break of throw.

He had six darts to take out 166 and 134 left him sitting on 32, but with Bristow on 76, Taylor missed three darts for the match.

Bristow hit treble 20, leaving him two darts at double eight – but he was off target, gifting Taylor another chance to clinch the match.

He missed double four, but found double two with his next dart and this epic match was over.

"Nothing compares to that," said Taylor. "To beat the big icon when he was playing well again and taking the mickey was something else. The final was a piece of cake after that."

The following night, Taylor walloped Priestley 6-3 in the final with a 100.92 average to equal Bristow's record of five World Championships and it would be 2003 before he would lose again at the Circus Tavern.

Two decades on from that semi-final, Bristow says he still watches the match.

"I turned up again and played well," he said.

"It was good for the crowd and people who love darts. They wanted to see me and Phil mix it. They didn't want to see a runaway job with me only winning a couple of legs.

"There were some good moments under pressure and that's what darts is all about. It's all about bottle. I didn't really choke. They were two good darts at double eight. I was unlucky.

"It was a battle, I made him work for it. You've heard of Custer's Last Stand? That was Bristow's last stand."

He never won another World Championship match.

Bobby George v Magnus Caris

NO. 11   1994 BDO World Championship semi-final

MOST of the talk before the 1994 BDO World Championship was about who wouldn't win it.

John Lowe wasn't coming back to defend his title and Eric Bristow wouldn't be in Frimley Green either; neither would Dennis Priestley, Jocky Wilson, Phil Taylor, John Lowe, Bob Anderson, Keith Deller and more.

They had broken away to form the World Darts Council and for the first time, there would be two World Darts Championships.

None of which seemed to bother Bobby George too much. He decided to stick with the BDO, but wasn't keen to take sides. Simply, he had no reason to make the switch to the World Darts Council where there was the promise of more tournaments and more prize money.

George made a good living without competitive darts – "I was doing a lot of work for breweries," he said – and it had taken a phone call from BDO boss Olly Croft to bring him out of semi-retirement for the 1993 World Championship.

He reached the semi-finals, where he was beaten by Lowe, and the following year, George was the most recognisable face in a championship that included debutants Martin Adams, Kevin Painter, Colin Monk, Roland Scholten and John Part.

His was a personality as big as any in the sport and, what's more, at a time of change and revolution, he was a link to the golden age of Bristow, Lowe, Wilson et al for BBC viewers to identify with.

George had battled them all, losing the 1980 World Championship final to Bristow, winning the News of the World Individual championship twice, and win or lose, he entertained.

He played to the gallery and the gallery cheered him on. They cheered when he nailed the double four that put him 2-0 ahead against Kevin Kenny in the quarter-finals of the 1994 World Championships.

"I went up in the air, came down and 'bang'!" said George. "Everything was out of place."

By 'everything' he meant his spine. "I always had back problems," said George, remembering his days spent laying granite floors and digging tunnels – and although he went on to beat Kenny 4-2, doctors ruled him out of the semi-finals.

"I had to go to hospital where they hung me upside down, carried out all sorts of tests and said I couldn't play," said George.

"They wouldn't give me any medication. If I had taken drugs, I wouldn't have felt any pain and would have carried on playing and hurt myself. I could have ended up crippling myself."

Nevertheless, the show (man) had to go on. "They made me a corset and said that would keep my spine straight and make sure I would stop playing before I hurt myself," said Bobby.

In the semi-finals, George met Magnus Caris and they had what Bobby would call "a bit of previous".

Caris had beaten George in qualifying for the 1988 World Championship – "I should have done him. I had three darts at double 18, missed and went out," remembered Bobby – and that result sent George into semi-retirement.

Not that it bothered him much.

All George was bothered about was "bees and honey" and if he made more "bees and honey" doing something other than playing darts, he would do that instead.

Reaching the semi-finals of the BDO World Championship in 1994 guaranteed him £7,700 and because of the injury to his back, he didn't expect to earn any more. "I thought I would just turn up and go through the motions," he said.

Caris was enjoying his best-ever World Championship.

In five previous attempts, he had never gone beyond the quarter-finals and to reach the final it looked like he would need to munch a few carrots.

"The lighting on stage was terrible," chuckled George years later. "I got my lighter out when we threw the practice darts. We were having a laugh. Eventually, they sorted the lights out."

His back was more troublesome…

"It really hurt," said George. "Every time I moved my head it hurt and every time I threw a dart it felt like a razor blade was being shoved up my arse."

Caris was rather more focused and only snapped out of his blank-eyed, open-mouthed trance to fling himself around the stage in joy whenever his darts landed in a double. It wasn't his celebrations that upset George, it was what he called "a bit of barracking".

"He was tapping his darts behind me," said George. "As I was throwing I could hear 'tap, tap, tap'.

"I told him, 'You can knock that on the head,' and I told the referee, Martin Fitzmaurice, about it.

"He apologised and said he didn't mean to do it. But there are players who will do anything to win. I've thought about doing a few tricks myself, but never have.

"He was beating me up, but after that happened I thought to myself: 'He's not beating me.'"

Caris should have beaten George.

From 2-0 down, he led 4-2 and in the seventh set, the Swede was just 141 points away from the final. His first two darts found treble 20 and treble 15, leaving double 18 for the match.

"He shouldn't have missed," said George, "but he thought about it.

"He thought: 'If I get this I'm in the final,' and his bottle went for that one dart.

"He must have been gutted. It could not have been any closer."

Caris was devastated, George transformed. He snatched the seventh set by nailing a do-or-die double 16 with Caris waiting on 32 for the match and took the momentum into the eighth set.

"Something happened to me," said Bobby. "I really did struggle with my back, but I forgot about the pain. I ploughed on and every time I went to the board I was hitting tons, 140s, doubles... I never missed.

"It was as though I had been hypnotised. I didn't think about playing in the semi-finals of the World Championship. I just threw the darts and they went in."

Caris had plenty to think about; there was that missed double 18, George snapping at his heels and then there was the crowd, previously appreciative of his efforts and now willing his opponent on.

"Bobby! Bobby!" they chanted and every treble and double George hit, they screamed it a decibel or two louder.

George, sweating heavily now, had found his rhythm. His darts were hitting the board harder than before and when he was off target, he kept his concentration and encouraged himself – "Come on Bo Bo" he would say – to make the next dart count.

For Caris, the agony went on. It seemed he couldn't chase the memory of that missed double 18 from his mind. His aim hadn't been the same since that match-winning chance was spurned – and George raced to the eighth set without reply to level at 4-4.

The crowd swept George towards the finishing line – "Gwaaan Bobeee!" they shouted – and he responded. From 4-2 down – and a dart at double 18 away from defeat – George won nine successive legs to pull off his greatest triumph.

"How do I feel?" he said afterwards. "It's like making love four times in a row."

Years later, he remembered: "After the game I was knackered. I had to leave the corset on and sit up in bed.

"I went to hospital and they said I couldn't play in the final.

"But if I hadn't played, Caris would have gone back in and if he had beaten [John] Part, he would have been world champion when I had already beaten him."

The miracles ended there.

George had his chances against Part in the final – but missed 44 of his 49 attempts at doubles and was whitewashed 6-0.

Part became the first overseas player to win the World Championship.

"I outscored him in every leg," said George. "I had no trouble throwing at the 20 and he was miles behind me. But I couldn't throw at the doubles on the left and right-hand side of the board because I couldn't move my body.

"If I could have hit my doubles, I would have won. I played well considering the state I was in. I was a cripple."

Chris Mason v Martin Adams

1999 BDO World Championship quarter-final

CHRIS Mason had darts in his DNA. His father Berkeley, a motor racing driver, and mother Margaret, who designed protective clothing for firemen, were both county players.

So were his brother and sister, while his uncle, Eddie Norman, sold darts equipment all over the world working for House of Darts.

"Darts was my life," said Mason. "All the other lads were into football, but I was mad about darts.

"I would come home from school when I was 11 or 12 years old and Eric Bristow would be in the living room practising with my dad. My mates didn't believe me when I told them."

At 16, Mason decided he would rather go to the gym and box than go to the pub and throw darts – it takes all sorts – but he wasn't lost to the game.

He returned to play Super League and county darts and with the financial help of a local pub landlord, Mason headed to the Belgium Open in 1994.

He lost in the semi-finals to Mike Gregory after having darts to win and remembered: "I was waiting backstage for the presentations to start and got chatting to this big guy whose English wasn't that great.

"I had the best banter I could have with someone who could hardly speak English and he told me: 'I will be world champion.'"

In 1998 – at the sixth attempt – Raymond van Barneveld did win the world title, reversing a loss to Richie Burnett in the 1995 final with a 6-5 win.

Mason bowed out in the second round, but his form during the rest of 1998 was good. He captured the Scottish and Dutch Opens, won the BDO Festival of Darts and was a semi-finalist at both the World Matchplay and World Masters.

At the Lakeside in 1999, Mason looked to be feeling pretty good about himself during wins over Ritchie Davies and Ted Hankey that took him through to the quarter-finals.

Where he met Martin 'Wolfie' Adams.

Both were regarded as very watchable talents who could sometimes lose matches they really should win.

This was a match Adams was fancied to win.

He recorded a championship-high average of 100.62 in his second-round win over Graham Hunt and had hit an impressive 47% of his doubles.

Mason's statistics were less impressive, but there was a feeling the longer match may suit him.

Often a slow starter, he had got better as the game went on against Hankey in the previous round.

The opening three sets of Mason–Adams went with the throw, leaving Adams 2-1 up.

The fourth set went to a deciding leg after Mason wired three darts at a double for 2-2.

Mason had the throw in the fifth leg, but again, his aim deserted him.

Adams pinched the darts off him with a well-timed maximum 180 and found double ten for a 3-1 lead with Mason sitting on 62.

"I couldn't believe I had lost the set," said Mason. "To come back from 3-1 down was a big ask. When you're behind, the pressure is doubled.

"I lost the fifth set as well through immaturity. I was just shaking my head, not thinking about what I was doing."

At 4-1 down, the match looked beyond Mason. "I thought I didn't have anything to lose," he said.

Mason had the throw in the sixth set, but Adams broke him and in the fourth leg, he had six darts to take out 161 for the match.

Adams missed the bull's-eye, then double eight and double four. He got another three chances to win the match – and missed them all.

Lisa Mason wept hysterically after her husband found the middle of double ten to save the match.

Mason had the darts in the deciding leg of the set – and there were signs the missed doubles were troubling Adams. The only trebles he could find with his first ten darts were treble one and treble five and Mason took control of the leg with a maximum 180. The crowd got behind Mason and the possibility of mischief put a glint in his eye and a smile on his lips as he took aim at 80 for the set. With his last dart Mason found double top for 4-2.

Still, Adams only had to hold his throw in either the seventh or ninth sets to win the match, but the way he was clumsily feeling for the match-winning double gave Mason the feeling all was not lost.

The crowd seemed to sense it as well.

Adams' seventh chance to win the match came and went in the fourth leg of the seventh set and with his last dart, Mason flung in double ten to pull off another dramatic escape.

In a high-scoring deciding leg, Adams and Mason matched each other treble for treble. Adams left 98 after nine throws and with Mason on 36, he needed to take it out. For the eighth time, Adams couldn't find the match-winning double, dragging his last dart into single 12 and Mason polished off an 11-darter to close the gap to a single set at 4-3.

And Mason had the darts to make it 4-4.

It seemed Adams could hit everything he went for apart from the match-winning double and that kept Mason going.

"Martin was pounding me," said Mason, "but he couldn't get over the finishing line.

"The more he missed, the more confidence I got. I started to believe I could win the match."

The eighth set – like the previous two – went to a deciding fifth leg and the pressure was on Mason to hold his throw to save the match.

Adams stole the darts off him and got to a finish first, leaving 76 for the match.

His third dart landed just inside double top and Mason found the same target with his first dart to force a ninth and deciding set.

Mason, who had nine times been a dart from defeat, broke in the second leg, leaving him a leg from victory.

Adams fought back. He finished 121 to win the third leg and started the next with six treble 20s. Unlike at the Norway and British Opens earlier in the season, he couldn't complete the perfect leg, but an 11-darter would do. That tied the scores at 2-2 and took the match into a tiebreak. The deciding set had to be won by two clear legs and if the scores reached 5-5, there would be a sudden death final leg.

The to-and-fro tungsten throwing went on.

Adams took out 105 to hold, Mason held for 3-3.

Mason broke in the seventh leg and in the next, he was a bull's-eye away from victory.

He missed, but with Adams way back on 160, it seemed likely Mason would be back for another shot.

From nowhere, Adams, surely just a couple of darts from defeat, somehow conjured up two treble 20s and a double top that meant this ding-dong duel went on.

"I thought: 'How did he take that out?'" remembered Mason. "I had him nailed."

Tony Green, commentating for the BBC, gasped: "I've seen every single dart in 22 years of the Embassy and I have never seen anything like this. This has had everything."

The ninth leg had another missed double from Adams – and three from Mason.

At the fourth attempt, Mason found the double for a break and a 5-4 lead.

That meant Mason would throw for the match in the tenth leg and if Adams broke, there would be a final sudden death decider.

Mason threw a maximum 180 – his 13th of the match – to leave 121 and Adams left the same.

Mason left 80, then Adams took his turn.

He missed the bull's-eye – and both kept missing.

"Pressure does funny things to you," said Mason. "Golfers talk about losing control of your elbow and it's the same with darts players."

Finally, a match that produced 29 maximum 180s came to an end when Mason put a dart in double one.

The relief overwhelmed him and he sank to his knees, while the crowd chanted: "Mason! Mason!"

"It was like a fight from a *Rocky* movie," said Mason. "Someone got in front, the other came back and we ended up scrapping it out at the end."

Phil Taylor v Adrian Lewis

2013 Grand Slam of Darts semi-final

PHIL Taylor calls this "the best match ever", Wayne Mardle agrees with him and if it lacked the dollops of seesaw human drama that makes darts so watchable, it had everything else...

More maximum 180s than any other PDC match, record averages...

For sheer quality, nobody expected to see a match that could equal the World Matchplay final between Taylor and Lewis in Blackpool that summer.

Taylor was an 18-13 winner at the Winter Gardens – despite 19 maximums from Lewis and a 105.92 average.

Mardle, as excitable in the commentary box as he had been on the oche, called it "the best match I have ever, ever watched".

Watching this match changed his mind.

As with most years, Taylor was the player to beat in 2013.

He had won the World Championship, the UK Open, the World Matchplay and the World Grand Prix.

Going into the semi-final of the Grand Slam of Darts, Taylor had won 25 consecutive matches in major televised tournaments, but he had been made to work for wins over Gary Anderson and James Wade that took him through to the last four at Wolverhampton Civic Hall.

In the group stages, Lewis had lost to Ronny Huybrechts, but victory over Christian Kist, the 2012 BDO world champion, earned him a place in the last 16 and averages of 105.24 and 100.16 secured wins over Michael van Gerwen and Kim Huybrechts respectively.

Lewis was possibly playing better than he did when he won the world title in 2011 and 2012 – and to beat him in the final in Blackpool, Taylor had to throw as well as he ever had.

Lewis threw more maximum 180s and more 140-plus scores, but Taylor's finishing was the difference and his match average of 111.23 lifted his tournament average to a career-high 106.28.

That win secured Taylor his sixth successive World Matchplay title – his 14th in total – and was his 43rd win in 54 matches against Lewis (one draw).

Their next match in front of the cameras was over the best of 31 legs in the semi-final of the Grand Slam of Darts.

Taylor struck an early blow.

Lewis had the advantage, but was soon under pressure after Taylor's first three darts brought him 180.

He added another on his way to winning the opening leg in 12 darts.

Taylor made a comment that had Lewis giggling before the start of the second leg and in the commentary box, Mardle sensed "a ploy".

"They seem pally, pally," he said. "I'm sure that's a Phil Taylor ploy. Disarm Adrian Lewis. Take away that needed aggression."

If it was a ploy by Taylor, it didn't work.

After 15 legs, neither had missed much, both had averages of more than 112.00 and Lewis was ahead 8-7.

Lewis had thrown 12 maximum 180s in the opening 15 legs – but throwing 180s at Taylor is unlike throwing 180s at anyone else. He doesn't get disheartened, he rises to the challenge.

"It's like a boxing match," Taylor has said. "They hit you and you have to hit them back."

Lewis said: "Phil always believes in himself. Whatever you throw, he believes he can match it or better it."

At 8-7, the bookmakers couldn't pick a winner. Both Taylor and Lewis were 11/10 on.

Lewis's 13th maximum 180 of the match couldn't prevent Taylor levelling the scores at 8-8 – and Taylor went on to break in the next by taking out 88 with Lewis sitting on 80.

Lewis missed two darts at double top to break straight back for 9-9 and just when it seemed he might get another shot, Taylor took out double five with his third dart for 10-8.

The 19th leg hurt Lewis more...

He was the width of the wire away from a 160 checkout, then watched Taylor take out the same treble 20, treble 20, double top finish to go three legs clear.

Even for a player of Taylor's calibre, that was some finish. The way Taylor was throwing, Lewis knew he couldn't afford to miss anything – not even a 160 checkout – because he was sure to be punished.

Lewis found himself 11-8 down having seemed certain to reduce the gap to 10-9 .

As is his way, Taylor twisted the knife.

He started the 20th leg with back-to-back 180s and although his seventh dart missed treble 20, Taylor went on to win a fifth straight leg for a 12-8 lead despite another Lewis maximum.

Lewis was throwing well enough to beat anyone – except Taylor.

"When Phil's hitting everything, you can lose focus and end up playing Phil Taylor instead of the dartboard," said Rod Harrington. "You end up thinking about what he's going to do."

That was what Taylor meant when he said he wanted to "get them [his opponents] thinking". That is, he wanted to "get them thinking about what I'm going to do next" and eventually "get them thinking they can't beat me".

Lewis didn't do that, however. He kept throwing 180s, kept getting down to finishes – and kept losing legs. In the 21st leg, he left himself 36 and watched Taylor take out 96, then threw another 180 in vain in the next.

Taylor won it in just 11 darts for 14-8 and he added the next with Lewis sitting on double four.

Lewis left himself double four in the 23rd leg as well – but Taylor took out 65 for an eighth straight leg that left him one away from the final.

By the 24th leg, Lewis knew his best wasn't going to be enough and he just shrugged and mustered a half-hearted salute to the crowd after another 180 flew in.

He did go on to win the leg, but Taylor grabbed the next – and the match – with Lewis sitting on a double after throwing a maximum, his 18th of the match.

Taylor threw 14 maximums himself in his 16-9 victory that took a breathless 52 minutes – making it a record total of 180s for a PDC match – and the combined averages was another best.

Taylor averaged 109.76, Lewis 110.99.

Lewis's average would surely have been enough to win any other match and afterwards he admitted the result had left him "in shock".

He had led 8-7, then got down to a finish of 100 or less in the next eight legs – and lost the lot.

"Every time I was on a double he went out on a big finish," said Lewis. "I've had ding-dongs like that on the floor over short formats, but never over that distance on television.

"If you average 111.00 you will win 99 per cent of matches."

He described the scoring in the match as "ridiculous" and Taylor said: "It was the best match ever. I didn't want it to end.

"It was magic, like a theme park ride where the louder you scream, the faster it goes."

For Taylor, there was another match to be played and won that night and he beat Robert Thornton 16-6 to win the Grand Slam of Darts for a fifth time.

Phil Taylor v James Wade

2010 Premier League final

2010 started much the same as any other year for Phil Taylor.

He won the World Championship for the 15th time at Alexandra Palace with victory over the extravagantly bearded Aussie Simon Whitlock, then went on to finish top of the Premier League after staying unbeaten throughout the 13-week season, dropping points only in draws against Mervyn King and James Wade.

King, Wade and a handful of others including Raymond van Barneveld had proved they could beat Taylor, but seldom did so.

He raised the bar beyond the reach of most of his rivals and on the rare occasions when someone else won a tournament, their achievement was devalued if they didn't beat Taylor on the way to lifting the trophy.

A legend that needed no exaggeration was exaggerated nonetheless.

Taylor's even better in practice, was an oft-heard whisper, he throws nine-darters for fun, hits a maximum 180 on the stroke of midnight every New Year's Eve...

During one event, Sky Sports attached wires to the players to monitor their heart rate and the high-tech equipment registered barely a ripple of nerves when Taylor took aim at all-or-nothing doubles.

More amusing was Alex Roy's claim that Taylor had broken wind at crucial moments during a World Championship match. He asked for Taylor to eat fewer Brussels sprouts before matches!

Another story went, Taylor could deliberately miss doubles, then find it with his third and last dart to hurt his opponent as much as possible, raising their hopes, then dashing them.

Could anyone really be that good? If anyone could be that good it was Taylor.

Wade had his successes against Taylor, including a victory on the opening night of the 2008 Premier League that was Taylor's first loss in the competition.

Wade was playing Taylor at the right time.

Taylor, unbeaten in 44 Premier League matches since the competition's opening night at the King's Hall in Stoke in January

2005, was tinkering with his tungsten after a quarter-final loss to Wayne Mardle in the PDC World Championship.

Wade beat him 8-6, but when Taylor's missiles were sorted out, he proved his point by reversing the loss in the finals of both the Premier League and the World Matchplay when there was much more at stake.

The latter match is remembered for some of the most jaw-dropping darts ever thrown, including what Sid Waddell described as "the greatest dart I have seen in 33 years watching the sport".

More of that elsewhere…

Wade had shown, if only occasionally, that he did have the game to beat Taylor – and the self-belief.

Back in May 1982, a floppy-fringed, teenaged Wade introduced himself to Jason Thame, then manager of Andy Jenkins, by saying: "You should sponsor me, I'm going to be world champion."

Wade, inspired by his grandmother to play darts, won his next event, the Swiss Open, and Thame agreed to manage him.

Although the World Championship had so far proved elusive, Wade went into the 2010 Premier League as the second most successful player in PDC history with four major titles, still way behind Taylor, of course.

His titles included the 2009 Premier League – ending Taylor's monopoly of the tournament after King beat 'The Power' in the semi-finals…

The 2010 Premier League had been set to reach its climax at Wembley Arena on a sunny Sunday evening in May, but an electrical fault meant the semi-finals and final had to be held the following night when, to the relief of tabloid headline writers, there was a 'Power' surge.

Taylor thrashed King 8-1 in the semi-finals – avenging his loss at the same stage 12 months earlier – after Wade had edged out Simon Whitlock 8-6.

Taylor spent the break before the best-of-19-legs final potting a few pool balls and playfully throwing punches at the Sky Sports commentary team, including Stephen Fry.

Fry, high-brow actor, comedian and author, had taken to social networking site Twitter to express his admiration for his darts heroes and was invited to sit alongside Sid Waddell and Rod Harrington in the commentary box for the semi-finals.

"I'm like a pig in Chardonnay," chuckled Fry and he correctly predicted finishes throughout Taylor's thumping of King.

Taylor averaged 107.98 against King – and looked to be enjoying himself as well. Commentators said they had never seen him look so relaxed before a big match in the minutes before the final.

Wade, however, was determined this final, unlike so many others before them, was not going to be the Phil Taylor Show. He launched the opening leg with a maximum 180 and went on to finish it with a 136 checkout.

Taylor rose to the challenge.

He started the second leg with throws of 174 and 180 to leave himself 147 points away from a nine-dart leg. Treble 20, treble 17 and double 18 completed the perfect leg.

The roar of the crowd made Wembley's walls wobble, while Wade stood at the back of the stage clapping his hands and trying not to think about what he had just seen. If Wade could concentrate on his own game, maybe he still had a chance… He had drawn with Taylor during the season, after all…

Taylor was looking unstoppable, however. He added the third leg with a 110 checkout and commentator Dave Lanning said: "If it goes on like this, it's likely to be the greatest darts match we've ever seen." During the interval, 'The Power' predicted another nine-darter before the end of the match.

Taylor, unable to hide his fury with himself when he occasionally did land a dart on the wrong side of the wire, went into that interval leading 4-2, soon made it 5-2, but he couldn't shake Wade off.

He would never, like others before him, settle for losing to Taylor by a respectable margin.

By holding his throw, Wade held on to Taylor "like a terrier" according to Fry and a break of throw in the 13th leg helped him level the match at 7-7.

For all his brilliance, Taylor could still lose the match and again, the challenge brought out the best in him.

He purposefully stepped up to launch the 15th leg with a maximum 180 – and followed it with another.

No player had ever thrown two nine-darters in the same match before. The crowd roared when Taylor stepped forward, then hushed themselves as he took aim at treble 20. "Yesss!" they hissed when his first dart went in – then treble 19 – "Go on!" – and finally double 12 brought an explosion of joy.

Incredibly, Taylor started the next leg with throws of 174 and 180 and another nine-dart leg – what would be the third of the match – was a possibility.

His seventh dart – a treble 20 – kept his hopes alive, but his eighth landed wide of treble 17. Playfully, the crowd booed. Taylor had raised their expectations so high that any miss was a disappointment, but he didn't miss any more darts in the leg and wrapped it up in ten throws.

At 9-7, Taylor was one leg from victory, but he missed three darts at double top in the 17th leg and suddenly, Wade, millimetres from defeat just moments earlier, was back in the match.

Wade won the leg to trim the gap to 9-8 and knew holding his throw in the 18th would take an astonishing match all the way to a deciding leg.

Few sportsmen respond to pressure better than Taylor, however, and he started the leg with another maximum, kept ahead of Wade and polished off the match with an 88 checkout.

He finished with a three-dart average of 111.67 – Wade averaged 100.08 – and as Stephen Fry handed Taylor the trophy he told an appreciative crowd: "Since the first Greek picked up a dart, it's never been done better."

Lanning, a darts commentator since ITV screened the News of the World Championship in 1972, described it as "the greatest darts match we've ever seen" and Taylor said achieving two nine-darters in the same match was "possibly the greatest moment of my career".

He added: "I don't think I can ever do better than this…"

EVEN the biggest darts fan – and there are some big ones out there – would have to admit the PDC World Cup of Darts wasn't the biggest event on the sporting calendar in 2012.

The Olympics came to London that summer and in Brazil, the football World Cup was staged.

Neither surpassed the World Cup of Darts for drama.

The Netherlands, represented by Raymond van Barneveld and Co Stompe, were the inaugural winners of the tournament in 2010, but two years later in Hamburg, they bowed out in the semi-finals to Australia.

The Australian pairing was Simon Whitlock, good enough to give Phil Taylor a fright or two in the 2010 PDC World Championship final, and Paul Nicholson.

Born in Newcastle-upon-Tyne, Nicholson grew up next to a pub and reckoned he was just three years old when he threw his first darts.

Childhood photographs showed him impersonating Jocky Wilson, but, as Nicholson grew older, the finger-stabbing Bob Anderson became his favourite player.

He loved Anderson's aggression and Nicholson, naturally a shy character, decided that was how he would bring the best out of his own game.

Nicholson wore sunglasses and a snarl and threw his darts as though he hated the board. He wasn't keen on his opponents either.

Pre-match preparations included giving opponents 'evils' across the practice room and when Nicholson got on stage he was in no mood to make friends with the crowd either. He glared at them and fired 'finger pistols' in their direction.

Very cool, very edgy, very unpopular. Nicholson delighted in turning the crowd against him, then shushing them after he hit the doubles.

If this was a mask, Nicholson didn't let it slip in post-match interviews he spent spelling out his belief that he would unseat Taylor and the rest.

Nicholson didn't just talk a good game. He threw one as well.

Nicholson, who emigrated to Melbourne in 2005 to live with his Australian wife Linda, won 15 titles on the Australian Grand Prix circuit in 2008 and within a couple of years of joining the PDC, he had beaten Phil Taylor in a televised tournament.

Doing what few players had done before, he then went on to win the 2010 Players Championship, beating Mervyn King in the final.

By the time the 2012 World Cup of Darts got under way in Hamburg, Taylor and Nicholson had plenty of history.

Perhaps their most famous altercation came at the UK Open in Bolton the previous summer when following Nicholson's dramatic last-leg win in the last 16, he appeared to wave Taylor off the stage.

In other exchanges, Nicholson called Taylor "a bully" and Taylor hinted at a fist fight to settle their differences.

Taylor and Adrian Lewis were on rather better terms. "Phil and I have a good chemistry," was how Lewis put it.

Lewis replaced James Wade in the World Cup team that headed to Hamburg where they were given a second-round scare by Canadian pair John Part and Ken MacNeil.

England – or Stoke-on-Trent – won the sudden death deciding leg and went on to reach the final.

Australia got there with wins over Ireland, Belgium and in the semi-finals, defending champions the Netherlands.

The winners of the World Cup would be the team that reached four points first.

A point was awarded for a win in each of the four singles matches, two for the doubles and if the team scores were level after that, the match would go to a sudden death final leg, as it did when England had played Canada.

Against Australia in the final, England won the opening three singles matches, meaning that if Lewis beat Nicholson over the best of 13 legs, he would win the World Cup for England.

Lewis would later say, "People don't realise what it means to you when you pull on an England shirt," and the pressure got to him.

For most of a poor match, Nicholson struggled to lift his average into the 80s, but it was still too much for Lewis and he won 7-4.

That left the match score 3-2 going into the doubles. Should England win the doubles, they would lift the trophy, but if Australia won, there would be a sudden death deciding leg.

Only a very basic knowledge of body language was required to know how Lewis felt about himself and his darts going into the decisive doubles match. Hands shoved deep in his pockets and shoulders hunched, Lewis waited to make his entrance with all the enthusiasm of a naughty schoolboy standing outside the headmaster's office.

Alongside him, Taylor shook himself loose and sang along to 'Roll With It' by Oasis in an attempt to lift himself – and Lewis – for one final push.

It didn't work.

The Aussies broke in the first and third legs for a 3-0 lead and though Taylor had finishes of 100 and 106, England couldn't get the breaks they needed and Whitlock sealed a 7-4 win for his country in style: taking out 124 on the bull's-eye.

That meant the match was going to a sudden death final leg.

The nearest the bull's-eye would determine who had the crucial advantage of the darts and after Taylor and Whitlock traded outer bull's-eyes, Taylor found the centre of the board with his fourth attempt.

England to throw first.

After 12 darts each, England had left 132 and Australia were on 156.

Taylor could take only 44 off England's score, then Whitlock's ton guaranteed Nicholson two darts at a double should Lewis fail to take out 88.

Lewis did fail to take out 88 – scoring just 32 – and Nicholson took aim at 56.

Nicholson thought he knew what high pressure darts was until this moment – and with the World Cup just a dart away, his nerve failed him. He missed double top with his second dart and put his last just outside double ten.

That gave Taylor a chance at 56 – and they thought it was all over.

It wasn't. He dragged his darts inside double 20 and double ten, surely gifting the World Cup to Australia.

The tension was too much for Lewis and Nicholson – they looked away – and, as it turned out, it was too much for Whitlock as well.

He was wide of double ten and double five, handing Lewis, the most nervous-looking of the four players for Sid Waddell, his chance to win the World Cup.

The others had all spurned theirs and while Taylor, Nicholson and Whitlock hung around the back of the stage looking sheepish and guilty, Lewis took a deep breath and stuck his first dart in the middle of double five with the minimum of fuss.

It was over now.

Lewis sank to his knees in relief, then, realising he had just won the World Cup of Darts for England, he picked himself up and hugged an embarrassed-looking Taylor.

Nicholson looked beyond devastated, told Sky Sports that Australia would win this trophy one day and went off to sulk for the next six months.

Martin Adams v Phill Nixon

NO. 6 2007 BDO World Championship final

A MATCH so exciting, so nerve-shredding that Mrs Martin Adams could hardly bear to watch it ...

For 13 years, she had watched her husband try and fail to win the BDO Championship and maybe this was his best chance.

Raymond van Barneveld thought so.

The four-time world champion had left for the PDC and, asked to pick a winner of the BDO World Championships in 2007, he reckoned all the talk about defending champion Jelle Klaasen and Michael van Gerwen would take the pressure off Adams, who clearly hadn't dealt with it too well in the past.

Two years earlier, Adams had come close, losing to van Barneveld in the final, and said: "I was going to keep trying until I won it. I knew it would happen one day, I just didn't know when. The World Championship is the one everyone wants to win."

For 20 years, Phill Nixon, an unemployed father of eight from County Durham, had just wanted to play in the BDO World Championship and when he finally qualified, cameras captured him locked in a private moment of clench-fisted joy backstage.

Nixon had World Championship experience of sorts having thrown darts on his board at home against whomever was playing on television and comparing scores.

Being unemployed for two years gave him more opportunity to practise "in between the hoovering".

The sniggers in the press room were silenced by wife Suzanne. "Don't think he wears a pinny at home," she said. "He does not."

Nixon did all the household chores, the press were told, apart from the ironing.

The press and public wanted to know more about Nixon, a 150/1 outsider for the title at the start of the World Championship, after he upset No. 7 seed Darryl Fitton, then seeds Martin Atkins (10), Paul Hanvidge (15) and Niels de Ruiter (11) to reach the final.

All of which surprised everyone – apart from Nixon himself. The night before he had set off on a ten-hour bus ride to Frimley Green, he had been asked at his local pub for his World Championship hopes.

"I'm not going there to lose," answered Nixon.

Pre-tournament favourites Klaasen and van Gerwen did lose in the opening round, to Co Stompe and Gary Robson respectively, and from the top half of the draw, Adams came through with wins over Tony O'Shea (3-0), Co Stompe (4-1), Ted Hankey (5-3) and Mervyn King (6-5) to set up what was known as 'The Centenary Final'.

Both Adams and Nixon were 50 years old, meaning the trophy would pass from its youngest winner in the championships' history, 21-year-old Klaasen, to its oldest.

That oldest-ever winner looked like being Adams.

He wrapped up the opening set against the darts with a 100 checkout and 44 minutes later was 6-0 up and just a set away from victory.

Nixon hadn't been missing by much, his darts were licking the wrong side of the wires, but Adams found the middle of just about everything he took aim at.

Adams could have done without the interval – "I probably would have won 7-0 without it," he said – and Nixon needed it desperately.

Suzanne Nixon found her husband in the players' room "throwing darts quite furiously into the board".

"He said something unrepeatable, finished his drink, had a cigarette and rammed his three darts into the side of his leg."

Nixon was telling himself: "Don't disgrace yourself."

"The worst thing I could think was that he would lose 7-0 and nobody would remember all the other games," said Suzanne. "It would just be the final that was talked about."

Only Dave Whitcombe (1986), Bobby George (1994) and Ronnie Baxter (2000) had suffered that embarrassment and after Adams re-emerged from the interval to launch the seventh set with 180, Nixon was well on his way to joining them.

Twice Nixon had to win a leg to stay in the match and twice he did it, taking out 112 in the fifth leg to grab the set.

Humiliation avoided, Nixon started to throw with freedom and 6-1 became 6-2, then 6-3.

"It was just us supporting Phill," said Suzanne, "but set by set, we could feel the whole room thinking: 'Can he do it?'

"Grown men were picking me up and throwing me around."

Maybe Adams was "running out of petrol" as Bobby George put it in commentary.

"It's hard to stop a player when they are on a roll," said Adams years later, "and when the Lakeside crowd see someone who's been struggling start to fight back, they will get behind them.

"I was pushing and pulling my darts and getting caught up in the atmosphere.

"I needed to stand back from it all, refocus and do what I would normally do. But that's easier said than done sometimes!"

In both the tenth and 11th sets, Adams pushed and pulled his darts wide when the World Championship was just a dart away and he was probably still thinking about his four missed match-winning chances while Nixon raced to the 12th set without reply to level the match. His face frozen in disbelief, Adams struggled to make sense of what had happened, while the television directors searched the crowd for joy and anguish in the faces of the players' loved ones.

They couldn't find Sharon Adams.

Previously, she had been shown dancing and jumping for joy as her husband's trebles and doubles flew in, but at 6-6 she disappeared.

"I was sobbing my eyes out in the toilet," she said afterwards. "I just could not bear to watch. Why does he always do this to me?"

Adams had tried to tell her "it is only a game of darts", but if anyone knew how much winning the World Championship meant to him it was Sharon.

Rather than "only a game of darts", Adams would later describe his quest for the World Championship as "an obsession".

Amid the chaos of his hysterical wife and the squandered 6-0 lead, Adams was somehow able to gather his thoughts.

"I just said to myself: 'Just play like you did in the first set and it will be a breeze,'" he remembered.

Nixon had the darts and while that was less significant in a deciding set that had to be won by two clear legs, at least it gave him the chance to take an early lead and put Adams under pressure.

But a maximum 180 from Adams in the opening leg shifted the pressure on to Nixon – and this time, he couldn't find a response.

Adams won the opening leg and after he held his throw in the next, Sharon, on the advice of the wife of the BDO official who had been helpfully pushing score updates under the toilet door, returned to watch him take out 54 for the match after Nixon had missed double 18 to save it.

After one hour, 58 minutes the match was over and Sharon ignored security to rush head down on to the stage and throw her arms around the new BDO champion of the world.

"It's the end of a 14-year dream, an obsession if you like," Adams told the press afterwards.

"I used to sit up every year and watch Eric Bristow. Now my name is on the trophy alongside him. I am part of darts history – but only just I guess."

For Nixon, it was back to reality.

"There were 30 people round at my house [watching the match] and I am going to have a real mess to clear up," he said.

The following year, Adams and Nixon were drawn together in the first round at Frimley Green – and Adams burst into tears after taking just 29 minutes to win 3-0.

In August 2013, Nixon died from cancer aged 57 and will be remembered for as long as darts are thrown.

"It's always the match people want to talk about," said Adams.

JOHN Part was a very, very good darts player – but he wasn't as good as Phil Taylor.

That much had been proved in 2002.

Part had reached the final of the World Matchplay and the World Grand Prix and both times, he lost to Taylor.

The loss in the World Matchplay final was from a winning position.

Part had led the best-of-35-legs match by a 16-15 scoreline, but Taylor took out 160 to level the match and pulled away to win.

"He stole the match from me," said Part, "but at least it showed I wasn't far away from him."

Part had always thought he was born to play darts.

His birthday was on the 180th day of the year – 29 June – and though Bob Sinnaeve was Canada's most recognisable darter in Part's youth, he preferred Bob Anderson's snarl and what he called his "trigger finger" that he stabbed at the board when his aim was true.

Part sought to bring similar aggression to the oche. "If you can be a Neanderthal on the oche that's quite good," he said. "There will be times when you have to think, like during the breaks, and you have to keep yourself feeling aggressive."

Part thought about darts, possibly too much at times. He felt he could talk and think his way into winning games, but also admitted: "Too much analysis leads to paralysis."

He was described by Mel Webb in *The Times* as "a Canadian of quite extraordinary erudition in the game that has its roots in the sawdust and spittoon milieu of the public bar" and nowhere was the reminder of darts' roots more obvious than amid the testosterone and tattoos of the Circus Tavern in Purfleet, where Taylor was unbeaten for eight years.

Part had made history in 1994 when he became the first overseas player to win the BDO World Championship, but just about every other record in darts belonged to Taylor, including his haul of ten World Championships, twice as many as his mentor, Eric Bristow.

In the 2001 World Championship final, Taylor had pummelled Part 7-0, restricting the Canadian to just three legs with an astonishing average of 107.58.

The *Guardian* described Taylor's performance as "ludicrous" and Part said: "He played to a standard that was unseen. If I had been beaten 7-0 by a 93 average, that would have been heartbreaking.

"But Phil's figures were unbelievable at the time.

"I felt bad, but it was such an excellent display that it took some of the hurt out of it.

"I made it inevitable in my mind that I would beat him in a major final one day."

The following year, Taylor and Part met in the quarter-finals and again, Part was whitewashed.

"I didn't resent Phil," said Part. "There were never any bad feelings. I just wanted to play at that standard. I just wanted to outdo him."

Taylor wasn't looking himself at the 2003 World Championship.

He had lost three stones in four months – there was talk he would enter the London Marathon – there were bottle blond highlights in his hair and a gold ring hung from his left ear.

The quality press took one look at Taylor and sniggered about "a Wham revival".

Sid Waddell, who at times seemed to know Taylor better than Taylor knew himself, wasn't convinced all of the above was a good idea.

He said losing all that weight so quickly had affected Taylor's balance and that he had "shown vulnerability" on his way to the final. Wayne Mardle and Dennis Smith did push him, but in the last four, Taylor thumped Alan Warriner 6-1, the perfect response to Warriner's pre-match promise to "sort him out".

Taylor would later admit he wasn't entirely happy with his form at the World Championship, however.

His darts weren't stacking as he would have liked and he was missing too many doubles.

Even so, he was confident of beating Part in the best-of-13-sets final.

He wrote in his autobiography: "I had the gut feeling John would never beat me in a major televised event."

Part had a different feeling. He remembers waking up in the early hours on the day of the final thinking: "I can win this, I should win this," although others wondered how much his gruelling wins over Jamie Harvey and Kevin Painter had taken out of him.

That semi-final with Painter went to a tenth set and if Part was going to beat Taylor in the final the following day, he would pinch his tactics.

Part won the nearest the bull's-eye and, just as Taylor often did, gave away the advantage of the throw.

"It's easier to break a guy in the first set," explained Part, "before he's found his game and built any momentum.

"In 2001, he gave away the throw, I missed double top for a 12-dart leg in the opening leg, he won it and went on to win 7-0.

"Two years later, I won the nearest the bull, then he missed a dart at double 16 for the first leg and I won it on 121.

"That was the first mental blow.

"He had put a stamp on the match very early [in 2001] and he never looked back.

"I tried to do the same."

To the astonishment of just about everyone, Part went 3-0 clear.

He said: "I did steam out and it did look like I could win 7-0 for a while."

Until Taylor won the fourth set against the darts after turning the set his way with a 122 checkout in the second leg.

Part broke back immediately to go 4-1 up and had the throw in the sixth set for a 5-1 lead that surely not even Taylor would be able to overturn.

When he had to, Taylor threw his best darts of the match.

He broke Part's throw in the third leg with an 11-darter and needed just 12 more darts to wrap up the set.

For the next three sets, Taylor hardly missed. He won the seventh and eighth sets without reply – wrapping up the seventh with a 109 checkout – to level the match and a 167 checkout in the fourth leg of the ninth set put him 5-4 ahead.

It was enough to break Part's spirit, but it didn't.

"People thought I was done for," said Part. "I knew it was going to be tough, but in stretches I knew I could outplay him and win more legs.

"I was confident I could get back into the match. I was playing very well and knew I had to just keep chipping away at it."

The tenth set went to a deciding leg and Part won it in just 11 darts. He was level again.

Taylor would later say he "suddenly felt very, very tired" in the tenth set and for whatever reason, he couldn't hold his throw in the 11th.

He made a mess of a 104 checkout for the set and Part took out 61, putting him 6-5 ahead and needing to hold his throw in the 12th set for the World Championship.

Taylor wasn't finished yet, however.

He broke in the first leg of the 12th set after a maximum 180 left 40 and went on to win it 3-1.

That meant that after two and a half hours, the longest World Championship final went into a 13th and deciding set.

Taylor had the throw, but couldn't keep it.

In the first leg, he had six darts to take out 89, but couldn't and Part found double 16 with his last dart to complete a 72 checkout and a crucial break of throw.

That gave Part control of the match. If he held his throw in the second and fourth legs, he would be world champion.

Part held in the second leg, then Taylor held his throw and if the fourth leg went with the darts, the match would be over.

Taylor needed a break to send the match into a tiebreak.

He did have a dart to save the match in that fourth leg, but missed the bull's-eye by a millimetre or two for a 121 checkout and, left 77 for the title, Part found 19, 18 and double top, then wheeled away to celebrate with all the uncoordinated joy of a schoolboy on the last day of term.

Taylor, in that decent way of his, led the applause.

"It was all about fighting and perseverance," said Part. "I knew after a couple of really rough experiences against Jamie Harvey and Kevin Painter, I had the stuff to stay in a tough match and I could get through it.

"I just kept throwing darts…"

Phil Taylor v Kevin Painter

2004 PDC World Championship final

PHIL Taylor retired from darts in January 2004 after winning his 11th World Championship.

"I will miss it, of course I will," he said. "Darts has been a massive part of my life and I love it. But I have to put my physical wellbeing and my family before anything else."

The match that convinced Taylor to walk away from darts was the gruelling PDC World Championship final against Kevin Painter.

Following that, he apparently thought about pursuing a possible career in pop music.

On *The Frank Skinner Show* he had dressed up in drag as Victoria Beckham to Skinner's David and sang the theme tune to Aussie soap *Home and Away* alongside pop stars Hear'Say and how Raymond van Barneveld, Colin Lloyd, John Part, Mervyn King et al must wish Taylor had stuck by his decision and changed careers...

Had Taylor retired, perhaps Kevin Painter would have benefited most of all.

Twice a quarter-finalist at the BDO World Championships, Painter announced his arrival in the PDC in the best way possible, by inflicting Taylor's first defeat in front of the television cameras for two years, in the first round of the World Grand Prix in 2001.

He was a semi-finalist at the World Championship two years later, but the good times didn't last and following a loss to Alex Roy in the first round of the World Matchplay a few months later, Painter was so disappointed, he thought about finding another way to pay his bills.

With his hair gelled and shoulders pinned back purposefully, Painter could have got a job working on the door at the Circus Tavern in Purfleet.

Instead, he headed there in December 2003 to play in the PDC World Championship – aggressively. "I play on the edge," he said once, while Dave Lanning described him as having "a gunslinger's gait" and he gunned down Paul Williams, Ronnie Baxter, Mark Dudbridge and Bob Anderson to reach the final.

In all four matches, Painter started fast. He won the opening two sets and against Anderson, he won the next four as well to complete a 6-0 whitewash. His three-dart average of 96.70 was his best of the championship, but going into the best-of-13-sets final, Taylor was a big favourite with the bookmakers at 1/12 after he dropped just four sets in wins over Colin McGarry, Dennis Priestley, Alan Warriner and Wayne Mardle.

Painter was a 6/1 outsider.

"I was playing brilliantly and didn't fear him," said Painter, "but I knew everyone expected me to lose. They all thought it would be 7-1 or 7-2 to Phil.

"I hadn't played him that many times – only four or five times – and apart from the match in Dublin, he had beaten me every time.

"But if you think about what Phil is capable of doing, you will fold. Phil is the only player you don't expect to beat, but being the underdog can help you relax."

Just as importantly, Painter said he had "never felt fitter" and against Taylor over a long distance, he reckoned stamina could be crucial.

"You have to keep hitting big score after big score and not many people can do that," he said. "You've got no chance if you don't get a good start and you have to stay with him in case he makes a mistake."

Twelve months earlier, Taylor had made mistakes. John Part ended his eight-year winning run in the World Championship with a nail-biting 7-6 win in the final and according to Sid Waddell, who knew him better than most, Taylor had thought of little else for the following 12 months.

Painter had been to the gym, Taylor had been to the curry house and at a venue where smoking seemed compulsory and according to Giles Smith of *The Times* the ceiling was so low "that under certain EU regulations it would probably only qualify as a table", there was the chance a long match may not suit Taylor, seven years older than Painter at 43.

Painter had the darts in the first set of the final and when he wasn't throwing them, he was looking at his shoes, trying to block out whatever Taylor was doing.

But he couldn't ignore the referee's roar of, "One hundred and eight-eeee!" that followed Taylor's third throw of the match and Painter knew the pressure was on when he took aim at a 136 finish for the opening leg.

Taylor was waiting on 60 and the way he was playing, was sure to take it out. Painter held his nerve to find treble 20, treble 20, double eight. "That first leg was crucial," said Painter and he went on to win the opening set.

He added the second set as well after Taylor wasted two chances to level the match, but Painter missed crucial doubles in the third set. He was off target with three darts at double eight for a 3-0 lead and Taylor pegged it back to 2-1.

It looked like a possible turning point.

Disappointment gnawed at Painter and while Taylor prepared to start the fourth set, 'The Artist' restlessly paced around the back of the stage trying to shake the memory of that missed chance from his head.

At such times, Taylor usually twists the knife, but couldn't find the crucial doubles and anxiously bit his flights in between throws while Painter pulled away into a 4-1 lead.

During the interval that followed, Taylor said the pressure was too much. He was going to quit. A few words from Eddie Cox, brother of manager Tommy, lifted Taylor and a few feet across the practice room, Painter had worries of his own despite his lead.

"Leading Taylor 4-1 in a best-of-13-sets match is unlike being 4-1 ahead against anyone else," he said. "You always know Phil has something to come back with. At 4-1 I told myself: 'Keep going, keep going…'"

Painter went on to open up a 5-3 lead – and he had the darts in the ninth set.

"I thought: 'If I have a good set here I could be in,'" he said. "But Phil played three of the greatest sets of darts to go 6-5 up. He started dancing on the stage. He had broken my throw and knew what it meant."

Taylor knew if he held his throw in the 12th set he would win the World Championship again.

But Painter won the opening leg against the darts and went on to send the match into a deciding 13th set.

Painter had the throw, but the deciding set had to be won by two clear legs, meaning he would still have to break Taylor's throw to win the championship. If the scores were level at 5-5 there would be a sudden death leg to decide the sport's biggest prize.

The chances – more half-chances really – went to Painter. He couldn't take out 160 for the match in the fourth leg and 124 in the sixth.

Both times he didn't get a dart at a double for the match – but he was on the brink in the eighth leg.

"I left 32 and thought: 'I've got a chance,'" said Painter, "but he took out 74 in two darts.

"Phil just doesn't feel pressure. Nobody else would have done that, but Phil is used to winning and he hates losing. He knows how to win games and pressure means nothing to him. He will take out 161 when you're sitting on a double. He knows how to hurt players.

"Players get a shot at a double and panic, but Phil isn't like that."

Both Taylor and Painter ignored the pressure and kept hitting doubles. At 5-5, the match went into a sudden death final leg – and after winning the nearest the bull's-eye, Taylor could only start with 45.

That left an opening for Painter, but he replied with 59. "I put my first three on the wire," he sighed years later. "If they had gone in…"

His darts kept missing the trebles and Taylor chipped away with scores of 100, 99 and a crucial 140 to leave him six darts to take out 117.

Taylor missed a dart at double top for the match, Painter chiselled his score down to 128 – and looked like he might get a chance to take it out as 'The Power' struggled to find the match-winning double.

He dragged his darts wide of double 20, then double ten and with the pressure at its nerve-jangling peak, Taylor nailed double five with his last dart and the match was finally won.

"I'm a very lucky man," said Taylor afterwards. "I just kept taking my chances and eventually he let me in."

He admitted later: "It was physical torture and the greatest night of my life all rolled into one."

Painter took positives from the loss.

"People think I must be devastated," he said, "but that game showed what I could do. I had arrived.

"I never had a dart to win it and if I had, I would have been world champion…"

Eric Bristow v Keith Deller

NO. 3   1983 BDO World Championship final

JOLLEES Cabaret Club looked no place for a 23-year-old teetotal mummy's boy...

Everywhere you looked through the cigarette smoke there were beer bellies, tattoos and testosterone.

Unless you looked in Keith Deller's direction...

Here was a milk-drinking goody two-shoes taught to play darts by his mother in the kitchen of the family home in Ipswich.

But even if he didn't look like anyone's idea of a darts player, for a year or more Deller had been throwing as well as anyone.

He won open events in Hastings, Suffolk and across the pond in Texas, Cleveland and Los Angeles.

That latest victory included wins over Bobby George, John Lowe and Bob Anderson and Deller went on to breeze through the World Championship play-offs.

Heading to Jollees in Stoke-on-Trent, only the cameras troubled him. Deller had never played on television before and secretly feared he would not be able to throw his best darts when the cameras were on him.

If he could deal with the spotlight's glare, Deller was sure he would win the World Championship. He had won most other tournaments he had entered – beating the best players along the way – and explaining his confidence years later he said: "You get used to being a winner. That's the important thing."

Deller told himself – and everyone else – the right things and so impressed was BBC presenter Peter Purves by his confidence, he bet £20 on Deller to become the first qualifier to win the World Championship at odds of 66/1.

George Bristow, Eric's father, was also showing an interest. Before every match, he checked on Deller's form and attitude in the practice room and backed him to beat Nicky Virachkul – "I don't lose to Americans," Deller had told him – and Les Capewell, then at longer odds, both John Lowe and Jocky Wilson.

The wins over Lowe and Wilson, both former world champions seeded Nos 3 and 2 respectively, left both George Bristow and his son smiling.

Eric would later admit the only players he feared were Lowe and Wilson – and Deller had eliminated them both.

"When he knocked John out I thought, 'That's handy,'" said Bristow, "and when he knocked Jocky out I thought: 'That's brilliant.'"

Bristow was "over the moon" to be playing the rookie Deller in the best-of-11-sets final. "I thought I would rip his head off," he said, but no matter what the odds against him, Deller found reason to be positive.

As an 18-year-old, he had twice beaten Bristow in exhibition matches in front of his home crowd in Ipswich and saw no reason why he couldn't do it again. "If I thought about playing the greatest player it would have been a negative," said Deller. "I just thought: 'I beat the No. 3 and I beat the No. 2, so why not the No. 1?' I was so confident."

Ten million viewers tuned in on Saturday tea-time to watch him try and Deller sensed most wanted him to win.

He reckoned that during the World Championship "the whole country started to get behind me", although George Bristow, understandably, had to change his allegiance for the final, no matter how tempting the odds.

Sid Waddell told the armchair enthusiasts that Deller was "not just an underdog, he's an underpuppy" and asked: "Can Deller do the unthinkable and beat Bristow in the world final?"

For Deller, who threw spring-loaded darts designed to avoid bounce-outs, reaching the final, a fine achievement for a qualifier, wasn't enough.

He was there to win the World Championship and predicted a 6-3 victory.

He blew six darts at a double to make it happen...

Earlier, the match had swung this way – Deller led 3-1 – then the other – Bristow levelled at 3-3 – then back again.

Deller won the seventh and eighth sets, taking him into a 5-3 lead and just one set away from the World Championship.

In the ninth set, Deller was 64 points away, then 18, then eight, then four...

Six darts at a match-winning double were missed and Deller spent the next two sets "shaking my head. I should have been world champion."

Ever the opportunist, Bristow showed why commentator Dave Lanning described him as "a burglar" on the oche.

In his youth, Bristow had burgled houses and the North London ne'er-do-well-turned-king-of-darts brought his street cunning to darts. Knowing Deller was vulnerable, his mind elsewhere, Bristow smoothly upped his average by a few points and plundered five legs without reply while Deller chewed over those missed match-winning chances.

When he claimed the opening leg of the 11th and deciding set, Bristow led for the first time in the match and that realisation, the possibility of defeat, snapped Deller out of his ruminations. Either he started throwing his best darts again or he would lose – and he hadn't come here to lose.

The spell broken, he rediscovered his fluency to break back immediately with a 121 checkout, then hold his throw to leave Bristow needing to do the same to save the match.

Bristow got to a finish first in that fourth leg.

He took aim at 121 with Deller also on a three-dart finish, 138.

Bristow threw 17, then treble 18 and with 50 left, everyone zoomed in on the bull's-eye. Everyone apart from Bristow, that is. Rather than go for the bull's-eye to win the leg, Bristow was so sure Deller wouldn't take out 138 for the match, he threw 18 to leave his favourite double 16.

This wasn't hubris. Bristow had thought it all through. He reckoned Deller's mental mastication – "He could have beaten me earlier, he had his chance" – and the awkwardness of the 138 finish – "it was all over the place" – guaranteed he would come back to the oche and have three darts at his favourite double.

Years later, he would think otherwise, saying the pressure would have been greater on Deller had he been faced with a smaller finish. "If he had 58 left he would have been standing behind me thinking: 'I've got two more darts for the title,'" he said, but still, nobody, not just Bristow, really expected Deller to take out 138.

"He's banking on Deller not doing this!" cried Waddell excitedly and when Deller's first dart landed in treble 20, there was a chance Bristow had got it wrong.

Deller had taken out big finishes in the earlier rounds of the championship and knew what he was doing. "I didn't stop," he said. "There was no way I was going to think about it."

Had he thought about the importance of the darts he was throwing, his arm would surely have twitched, so Deller ignored the crowd's growing excitement when he nailed treble 18 and coolly switched across the board to fire his final dart into double 12.

"I have never seen anything like it in my life," said Waddell while Deller shook his fists above his head in sheer joy.

"It was perhaps the next best thing that could happen to me," Deller would tell *Darts World*, "... next to playing for Ipswich Town."

Presumably, being photographed in bed with a pair of page three girls would feature somewhere near the top of that list of 'Best Things That Could Happen To Keith Deller' and that also happened in the days after he beat Bristow.

And there was more...

"People say: 'What difference did it make to you, winning the world title?'" said Deller. "I say: 'I had no money at all and three months later, I bought a house in London with a swimming pool.'"

Phil Taylor v Mike Gregory

1992 BDO World Championship final

ASK Phil Taylor to name his favourite match and he will give the same answer as many others...

Doubtless Mike Gregory has another favourite.

The 1992 BDO World Championship final was the match that gave him six chances to change his life – and he didn't take them.

Gregory had been throwing darts most of his life – he was just four years old when his step-brother introduced him to the sport – and reckoned he had never thrown them better going into those World Championships.

"I always thought I was the best player," he said. "I just had to go out there and do it."

According to the seedings, he was the second-best player, behind Taylor, the champion in 1990.

Gregory had been a consistent performer at the World Championship. He was a semi-finalist in 1990, losing to Eric Bristow, and Jocky Wilson had beaten him three times in the last eight.

Gregory was determined to go further and to prepare for the 1992 championships he erected a stage in the living room of his Bath home in a bid to recreate the atmosphere at the Lakeside Country Club, while Taylor rearranged things between his ears before he headed to Surrey.

He won the title in 1990, thrashing mentor Bristow in the final, and 12 months later, his defence had ended in tears.

"I thought I just had to turn up to win it," said Taylor, explaining a quarter-final loss to Dennis Priestley. "But I got everything right in 1992. I got my head right."

Second-round defeats for defending champion Priestley and Bristow – to Martin Phillips and Alan Warriner respectively – cleared the way for the top two seeds to reach the final.

Gregory was taken all the way to a seventh and deciding set by Rod Harrington in the quarter-finals and Taylor had to come through a titanic, nine-set semi-final against John Lowe. His nail-biting 5-4 win meant that for the first time since the World Championships started in 1978, neither Lowe nor Bristow would appear in the final.

Although tired by his semi-final epic, Taylor was thinking positively. "I could relax," he said. "It had been a hard week, I had done the hard work by reaching the final and was on a good payday."

Taylor and Gregory knew each other well. They had practised checkouts together and Taylor rated Gregory as "the best finisher I ever played with". How ironic...

For their final over the best of 11 sets, Gregory made changes.

"I practised to slow down a bit and concentrate on every dart rather than trying to get into a rhythm," he said. "Phil had been hammering everybody, but I thought that if I got in quick and was consistent I would be fine."

Taylor was also confident. "I thought I was going to batter him," he laughed years later.

For two sets, Taylor did batter Gregory, but he drew level, then went 3-2 ahead. The seesawing continued until Taylor held his throw in the deciding leg of the tenth set and that meant the World Championship final would go to a deciding set for only the second time in the tournament's history.

The drama was only just beginning...

Gregory won the opening two legs, but with the title just a few well-thrown darts away, he couldn't break Taylor's throw or hold his own and at 2-2 in the deciding set, the match went to a tiebreak. "The match has to be won by two clear legs," said referee Bruce Spendley.

The first match-winning chance went to Gregory in the sixth leg. He left himself 61 and treble 15 with his first dart landed him on double eight. His attempts landed just outside the wire – and just inside the wire.

Taylor saved the match with double five with his last dart, the crowd screamed and although known as 'The Quiet Man', Gregory showed his feelings. His shoulders sagged and his face was twisted in anguish and disbelief. Why wouldn't this double go in like all the others had?

"It was just excitement," said Gregory years later.

"You get excited when you're that close to the winning line. I think I rushed a few of the shots." Still, Gregory held himself together and went on to fashion more match-winning opportunities – and he kept missing them.

His next chance came in the tenth leg. His attempt at double 20 was wayward, but Taylor's failure to take out 116 handed him three more darts at a match-winning double. Gregory's radar – so finely tuned in for much of the previous ten sets – went on the blink again when the World Championship was just one good dart away. His first dart was dragged into the single 20 and his two attempts at double ten landed agonisingly just outside their target.

Six darts at a match-winning double had now been missed. Gregory had entered what he would later call his 'Bermuda Triangle' – where his doubles went missing – and Taylor sensed a chance. He remembered: "I noticed that when he threw to win the match he was snatching. I thought: 'If I get one shot I'm going to bang the double in.' I just thought: 'Please give me one shot.'"

Almost apologetically, Taylor nailed double top to level the deciding set at 5-5 and with that, the World Championship final went to a sudden death leg for the first time.

Taylor remembers telling himself: "All the hours of practice, all the hard work, do it now for this one leg."

Again, Gregory pulled himself together well enough to win the nearest the bull's-eye – he could hit just about everything he aimed at apart from the match-winning double, it seemed – and just when he thought things couldn't get any worse, they did.

His third dart of the leg smacked against the wire above the treble 20 and ended up on the floor, reducing his score from a possible 140 to just 80. This was the chance Taylor had been waiting for and he stepped in with back-to-back 140s to take charge of the leg. That helped him get to a finish first and he fired in double top to win the title with Gregory waiting on 60.

Taylor, in that decent way of his, didn't celebrate, he just sighed and reached to shake Gregory's hand. He later told Gregory: "We should never have played that last leg, then we could have kept the trophy for six months each."

Gregory, his head bowed and shoulders hunched, told television viewers afterwards: "All I wanted was a shot. I missed and he took the title."

Those missed doubles cost him the title, £14,000 – Taylor scooped £28,000 for winning his second world title – and many thousands more over the years. As world champion, Gregory could have raised – perhaps even doubled – his exhibition fee and still expect a full diary. As a leading player, he still got bookings, of course, and remembered: "The weird thing is, the first exhibition after losing to Phil I left 76 and hit double eight, double ten and double 20 sweet as a nut. Why couldn't I do it then?" Millions enjoyed the edge-of-the-seat drama of the sudden death shoot-out – apart from those tuning in to watch the BBC's coverage of Crufts, which was due to start.

Viewers had to wait for the darts to finish.

"It went mental," said Taylor. "Everywhere I went people wanted my autograph.

"Everyone loved that game and people still ask me about that final. It was the best final ever and when I get in a tough situation I've thought: 'I've done this before against Mike.' It helped me in other matches when I had to dig deep to get through."

Struggling to find a positive, Gregory managed a smile and muttered: "At least I didn't have to polish the trophy."

Phil Taylor v
Raymond van Barneveld

2007 PDC World Championship final

PHIL Taylor and Raymond van Barneveld didn't hate each other. They hated losing. "It kills me," admitted Taylor once – and van Barneveld said: "Ever since I was young, I could never handle losing.

"I played board games with my mother and father and if I lost, I would throw the board on the floor.

"My attitude has always been: 'Win, win, win, never lose' and I don't know where it comes from. My parents aren't like that at all.

"No sportsman likes to lose, some players handle losing better than others, but they will never be world champion. Some players are just pleased to qualify for tournaments and I can't believe that.

"If I lose at a major tournament, I go to my hotel room and shut the door. I don't want to hurt people by saying the wrong thing. You are better off not texting me after I've lost. You won't like the reply!"

For Taylor and van Barneveld, winning was everything and the sheer quality of their duels meant every pilot, sailor and Viking among the colourful and often distracted darts audience watched, oooh'd and aaah'd along with every twist and turn as 'Barney' showed he could dig just as deep as 'The Power' in the do-or-die legs.

Taylor and van Barneveld pushed each other on to hit higher scores, take out bigger finishes and incredibly, their opening five matches in the PDC all went to a deciding leg. Taylor won twice, van Barneveld won twice and their other match was drawn.

No match between them would ever be more dramatic than the 2007 PDC World Championship final.

But the biggest match in darts almost never happened.

Had Colin Lloyd showed a truer aim in the second round, van Barneveld would have been heading home. But 'Jaws' missed four darts at a match-winning double and van Barneveld snatched a place in the last 16 by winning a sudden death deciding leg.

Taylor's career – not just his tournament – looked like it could be over after his third-round match with combustible Chris Mason.

By the time he met Taylor, Mason was an unfulfilled talent. As television commentator Sid Waddell put it: "He's got a great future behind him" – and the frustration was starting to show.

Mason branded Taylor "arrogant" and "patronising" before their match and said that by arriving for the championship in a Bentley, Taylor was "rubbing people's noses in it".

Taylor answered with a 4-0 win and a few post-match comments.

"If they are going to be like that, don't invite me," he said. "I'll just walk away. Keep the game. I don't want it. I'm sick of it. I won a game of darts, turned to shake his hand and he effed and blinded at me."

Mason scribbled a letter of apology and Taylor went ahead with his quarter-final against Darren Webster. He won 5-1, then walloped Henry VIII lookalike Andy Hamilton to maintain his record of reaching every final of the PDC World Championship since it started in 1994.

After his second-round scare, van Barneveld, his nerves calmed by meditating twice every day, went on to whitewash Rico Vonck, Alan Tabern and Andy Jenkins to reach the PDC final at the first attempt.

Between them, Taylor and van Barneveld had won 17 world championships – Taylor's share was 13 – and more than one million viewers on both sides of the North Sea tuned in to watch the best two players on the planet compete for the sport's biggest prize. Closer to the action, darts fans, sensing one of those tell-your-grandchildren nights, squeezed into every smoky, sweaty corner of the Circus Tavern to catch a glimpse of the action.

Both players had their supporters among the crowd and Taylor dressed like one of van Barneveld's fans.

His supporters wore the orange of the Dutch national football team – and so did Taylor.

Perhaps unsettled by Taylor's mind games, van Barneveld took ten darts to find a treble 20 and left the stage at the first interval having won just one leg in the opening three sets.

"I just didn't turn up," he said. "I wasn't there.

"My manager came to the side of the stage and said, 'Come on Raymond, you can do it,' and then it became a game."

At the interval, bookmakers made van Barneveld a 33/1 outsider to overturn the 3-0 deficit in the best-of-13-sets match – and he doesn't remember much of what happened next.

All he can recall is being 3-0 down at the interval – then 6-5 ahead. He would later say he must have been in a trance throughout those eight sets of magical, seesaw darts.

If he watches a recording – or better still, reads this book – van Barneveld will discover that in the opening leg of the fourth set,

Taylor chucked three misbehaving missiles that brought only 26 and handed him a chance to break the throw.

'Barney' took it and went on to wrap up the set with a maximum 170 checkout.

The match was on.

Van Barneveld still needed another break of throw to overhaul Taylor's lead, however, and going into the tenth set, he was running out of time.

Taylor led 5-4 and only had to hold his throw in the tenth and 12th sets to win the match.

But like all great champions, van Barneveld believes no cause is ever lost. He got the break he needed to level the match at 5-5, then held his throw in the 11th set. From being 5-4 down and heading for defeat, van Barneveld was now 6-5 ahead and three legs away from the world championship.

Taylor had to hold his throw in the 12th set to save the match and didn't look like doing it.

Breaks of throw in the first and third legs took van Barneveld to the brink. He threw for the championship in the fourth leg, but Taylor broke with a 12-darter, then held his throw to send the match into a deciding 13th set.

Although he had the darts, van Barneveld would still have to break Taylor's throw because the deciding set had to be won by two clear legs and if the score reached 5-5, there would be a sudden death final leg.

Van Barneveld got his chance in the fourth leg, but missed a dart at double top and another match-winning opportunity was wasted in the sixth leg.

Left 40 for the match, van Barneveld was off target with two attempts at double top and another at double ten.

He was in agony, but held himself together to keep matching Taylor treble for treble, double for double. Every dart mattered now. Both knew if they threw poorly, they were sure to be punished. Neither gave any ground.

Van Barneveld held his throw, Taylor held his and at 5-5, the match went into a sudden death final leg.

Taylor and van Barneveld had been inseparable after more than three hours of darts and 110 seesaw legs – they had won 55 apiece – and the crowd willingly put down their pint glasses and stood to applaud them before they took aim for the bull's-eye to decide who would throw first in the final leg.

Waterstones

Waterstones
153-157 Sauchiehall Street
Glasgow
G2 3EW
01413329105

SALE TRANSACTION

DARTS GREATEST GAME	£10.01
9781785313004	
CARRIER BAG - SCOTL	£0.05
2000006907882	

No. items 2
Balance to pay

£17.04

Gift Card Tendered £17.04

- - - - - - - - - - - - - - - -

WATERSTONES REWARDS POINTS
CARD NUMBER: **** **** **** 2040
Total qualifying spend
Start Balance   3815
Earned This Visit   51
Your Current Balance   3866
Your Points are Worth   £38.66
   Points will be credited to your
   account within one working day

- - - - - - - - - - - - - - - -

Waterstones
VAT Reg No. GB 108 2770 24

STORE	TILL	OP NO.	TRANS.	DATE	TIME
0085	8	811563	197440	10/08/2017	10:11

□999020006   9744060

We will happily refund or exchange
goods within 30 days or at the manager's
discretion. Please bring them back with
this receipt and in resalable condition.
There are some exclusions such as Book
Tokens and specially ordered items, so
please ask a bookseller for details.

This does not affect your statutory rights.

Waterstones Booksellers,
203/206 Piccadilly, London, W1J 9HD.

Get in touch with us:
customerservice@waterstones.com
or 0808 118 8787.

Buy online at Waterstones.com or Click & Collect.
Reserve online. Collect at your local bookshop.

Did you love the last book you read? Share your
thoughts by reviewing on Waterstones.com

Waterstones

Refunds & exchanges

We will happily refund or exchange
goods within 30 days or at the manager's
discretion. Please bring them back with
this receipt and in resalable condition.
There are some exclusions such as Book
Tokens and specially ordered items, so
please ask a bookseller for details.

This does not affect your statutory rights.

Waterstones Booksellers,
203/206 Piccadilly, London, W1J 9HD.

Get in touch with us:
customerservice@waterstones.com
or 0808 118 8787.

Buy online at Waterstones.com or Click & Collect.
Reserve online. Collect at your local bookshop.

Did you love the last book you read? Share your
thoughts by reviewing on Waterstones.com

Waterstones

Taylor had twice won sudden death shoot-outs in World Championship finals – against Mike Gregory in 1992, then Kevin Painter 12 years later – and would have to do it the hard way against van Barneveld after surrendering the advantage of the throw.

He started with 100, Taylor replied with 180 and it looked decisive. "I thought I had the bugger," Taylor said later.

Van Barneveld had to respond with his next three darts or Taylor would surely pull away and win. Van Barneveld threw treble 20… treble 20… treble 20. They had to be the best darts he has ever thrown and they piled the pressure back on Taylor.

He took a deep breath before taking aim. It was all or nothing now. At such times, Taylor usually had more inner steel than any other player, but not this time.

He could score only 40, leaving him way back on 281 and needing at least six darts to finish.

Van Barneveld threw 105 to leave 116 and would surely get a shot at a double first.

To have any chance, Taylor needed a big score and 133 left him a finish of 148 – if van Barneveld missed.

He did miss. He was millimetres too high with a dart at double top to complete a match-winning 116 checkout.

Taylor had a chance, half a chance really. The 148 checkout was beyond even him – he left himself 90 – and the focus shifted to van Barneveld.

Wife Sylvia couldn't bear to watch – van Barneveld had already missed four darts to win the match – but the crowd's roar told her he nailed double top at the first attempt this time.

"There's no better feeling than beating Phil Taylor in a world final," said van Barneveld. "Not many people can say they've done that."